The advanced guide to
Floristry

The advanced guide to

Floristry

ROSEMARY BATHO
STEPHEN ROBERTS
BERNICE WAUGH

MEREHURST

Contents

Introduction   6

DECORATIVE ARRANGEMENTS   10

SYMPATHY DESIGNS   36

FLORAL WEDDINGS   56

IDEAS FOR HANDTIEDS   76

SPECIAL EVENT SCHEMES   98

EXTENDING THE BOUNDARIES   124

Cut Flower Care   144
Techniques   152
Index   158
Acknowledgements   160

Exploring floristry

The excitement of working with the breathtaking and beautiful flowers that are currently available never fails to amaze and delight. Incredibly, the range expands continuously, and almost every day there is a new flower, a subtle colour, or a novel technique to add to the already-bursting palette of colours, textures and forms. The focus of this advanced guide to floristry and flower arranging concentrates on the influences and changes that occur constantly in the industry.

Floral design has always been affected not just by nature, but also by developments in other design fields, including art and fashion. The study of paintings and sculpture can help a designer to develop an informed understanding of composition and colour, of form, proportion and a sense of the dramatic. This can be used to advantage with a florist's sense of occasion, providing imaginative designs for weddings, gifts and special events. Styles can develop from fashion trends, whether lacy and flouncy or simple and sophisticated. Florists and flower arrangers are also experimenting with new and interesting ideas generated from our current awareness of the environment and nature, and the outdoors can provide an important stimulus and inspiration. For example, recent developments in British

landscape and garden design have incorporated distinct influences from Europe, while retaining the essence of its own traditions and its use of the abundant plant material available in a temperate climate.

A CREATIVE ENVIRONMENT

As the nations of the world draw closer together, the cross fertilization of ideas is producing richer and more varied floral designs than ever before. For example, the Dutch use of plant materials, the German and Scandinavian sense of design, and the Italian and Spanish flamboyance can all be combined with British design approaches. Building on experience from several parts of Europe, the three authors have worked together as a design team, exploring techniques and testing theories in their day-to-day work at the Welsh College of Horticulture. Overlooking the picturesque Dee estuary, the authors work alongside students in extensive grounds, over 200 acres in all, much of which is ornamental landscape.

Flowers and foliage are often a major source of inspiration in the creation of a floral design, but emotions, moods, patterns and a myriad of other influences stimulate the creative flow and excite the senses.
Here are three very different arrangements, each showing ways in which basic design principles can be exploited.

The gardens and wild areas are a natural resource that can be used to expand technical skills and design concepts. Individual and group experimental work allows the thoughtful analysis of growing habits and the re-creation of the natural movement of plants in floral designs. The landscape department has recently created a grass garden, and this new area complements other distinct and varied plant habitats that are equally useful in providing study examples of the conditions in which particular plants thrive.

Materials such as leaves, branches, stems and moss are used in innovative ways to allow creative talents to have free rein. Exciting structures, designs and bouquets are constructed using the skills gained from and influenced by this natural countryside environment. Imaginative skills and evolving design theories are explored, explained and illustrated in these pages. These influences are an integral part of teaching at the Welsh College.

DESIGN INSPIRATION

Each chapter looks at a section of the work that is undertaken by florists today. Each design project, whether it is an arrangement, bouquet or sympathy piece, is broken down into the stages of development leading to the finished product. The reader is shown the inspiration behind the design, and follows the process of construction. Alternative flowers, foliage or containers have been suggested, and the text finishes with a practical professional tip that is particularly relevant to that design.

The book begins with flower arrangements, each featuring a new technique or a fresh approach to designing, and encouraging the reader to look at each particular type of arrangement with new eyes. Decorative arrangements give way to sympathy tributes, illustrating interesting ways of using flowers and foliage, ranging from weaving to designs that can be adapted to other types of floristry. The wedding chapter examines the most popular aspects of a florist's work, and contains a wealth of stunning and unusual bouquets to whet the appetite and inspire further designs. A range of ideas is then illustrated for handtied designs, from lead-wrapped bouquets to spiralled and woven creations. The special events section deals with those occasions when something special is required and considerable thought and creative flair must be put into the design process. A children's party, for example, will require a completely different approach to that needed by a successful design for a business function. The final chapter, Extending the Boundaries, opens up a range of experimental concepts that will hopefully prove inspirational for the adventurous.

All of these vital studies are the backbone of a creative approach that will guide the next generation of florists.

LEFT A subtle combination of textures gives this design its distinctive quality.

RIGHT Style, varied textures and a superb selection of materials make this wedding bouquet a stunning design for a special bride.

Decorative arrangements

Colour palettes

Today, more than ever before, a marvellous array of colours is available in flowers and foliage, ranging from the palest hint of pink to the deepest crimsons, from dull golds to rich browns, and from vivid blues to the softest mauves. There is even an increasing range of green flowers, such as *Gladiolus* 'Woodpecker', *Zinnia* 'Envy' and a host of orchids, hellebores and arums. Finally, a beautifully-formed small black rose – 'Black Bee' – is now available. All of these ensure that we have a full palette of colours at our disposal when designing with flowers.

COLOUR RESPONSES

If the recipient of one of the arrangements in this section were asked at a later date what he or she particularly remembered about the design, colour would almost certainly be the dominant recollection – the striking yellow of the arum lilies, perhaps, or the delicate pink and white colours of the Mother's Day gift. Emotive and personal, colour is the most exciting and demanding element of design, and understanding its nuances and uses is an essential part of the expertise of any successful floral designer.

Certain combinations have feminine or masculine connotations. Neutral colours and earthy tones or bright colours, such as red, yellow and orange, tend to be associated with men, for example, while feminine colours reflect the personality of the woman. The stereotypical feminine colours are delicate pastels, but

An exhuberant palette of colours can be seen in this homage to the Flemish old masters.

the chic woman of today is more discerningly colour conscious and often relates to colour trends.

Young people are often attracted by bright, intense and energetic colours, including vivid red, clear oranges, sharp yellows and bright blues. The older generation enjoy cheerful colours, but they also respond to soft tints and pastels. Remember that people with poor sight will appreciate the bright advancing red, yellow and orange colours.

Strong superstitions are attached to certain colours. The combination of red and white, for example, is strongly disliked by hospital nursing staff, as it is supposed to signify death. Many consider green to be unlucky, and some clients will prefer that their handtied or flat-backed bouquet is not tied with green ribbon. Purple ribbon and white lilies have long been associated with funerals, but this old tradition is gradually fading.

THE APPROPRIATE COLOUR

For large parties, use bold, striking colours. Exciting complementary colour harmonies, such as blue and orange or yellow and violet will demand attention and interest. The colour combination for a dinner party, on the other hand, must be chosen to blend or contrast with the table linen, napkins, china, cutlery and glass. Remember that as well as being decorative, a floral arrangement should also be a topic of conversation, and this will be achieved by the clever use of colour.

LEFT The orange of the parrot tulips and the purple of the freesias to the left is a combination of colours that is exciting and eye-catching.

BELOW is a subtler and softer approach, using golds, creams and lime greens that are adjacent on the colour wheel.

Avoid selecting vivid colours, such as acid yellow or aggressive red, for hospital designs, as these can be visually tiring for the patients. A selection of flowers that share the same intensity of colour can make people feel ill. For example, pure yellow roses, freesias and acid yellow carnation sprays mixed with mimosa could have this effect. Instead, select warm colours, such as golds, creams, or oranges and peaches, mixing these with the stabilizing influence of green, which will be easy to look at and gentle on the eye.

There will always be certain colour combinations in vogue. These can vary from the rich jewel colours of emerald green, sapphire blue and ruby red, to the vivid colours of hot fuschias, reds and pinks or the demanding lime greens, clear oranges and pushy purples. If vivid colours are in fashion, it is highly likely that the following year will see a return to peace and tranquillity as fashion dictates that creams, pale pinks and soft greens are the new season's colours.

SEASONS AND SPECIAL DAYS

Colours play an important part in church festivals. For Advent and Christmas, red and green (holly and berries) are also traditional favourites, but golds, whites, yellows, and oranges with variegated foliage are now being used. Easter could be celebrated with yellow daffodils and white lilies. Yellows, oranges, browns and dark red are the traditional colours for a harvest festival or Thanksgiving. Other festivals include St Valentine's Day. Romantic reds are the classic choice here, but the more adventurous find that rich golds, startling whites, greens and mysterious blues can be equally romantic. Children love bright flowers for their mums, so a kaleidoscope of colours, including yellows, violets, pinks, peach and oranges, are all suitable for a special Mother's Day.

Cornucopia

The cornucopia, or horn of plenty, was the inspiration for this waterfall-style design. The horn of plenty is an image that occurs time and time again in classical art. It typifies the abundance of nature, particularly the harvest time of the late summer and early autumn. Containers of this shape are traditionally made of wicker or woven willow, but here the soft patina of the lead wrapping allows a choice of plant materials from the cool side of the colour wheel not normally associated with abundance. The lines of the container and plant materials complement each other, strengthening the curvilinear shape of the overall design. Notice how the upward curve of the end of the cornucopia is repeated at the tips of the plant materials.

CHOICE OF MATERIALS

Two main selection criteria were used while hunting for the materials for this design. Foliage and flowers needed to have soft natural curves which would allow the plant materials to flow out of the softly-curving cone. The colour link with the lead of the container was also important. The deep green of the large leaves of *Anthurium andreanum* and the dark rich purple *Trachelium caeruleum* flowers give this design a solid look, and stop the heavy container dominating the plant materials. The *Trachelium* is light and feathery in form, however, and this, with the finer foliage of the palm fronds, lifts the design, while the pure white flowers of *Clematis montana* variety, 'Grandiflora', finish the selection.

ALTERNATIVE FLOWERS

Agapanthus 'Donau' and the feathery *Aster* 'Blue Butterfly' would combine beautifully to give the natural, sweeping lines required for this design.

A metal rod will support long trails of Clemetis montana and enable them to retain the required elegant curves.

CONSTRUCTION METHOD

The container is made from thin lead sheeting wrapped in a spiral around a pre-formed wire shape. A bowl filled with plastic foam is then placed at the mouth of the cornucopia. To secure any long trailing pieces of plant material, a thin metal rod is bent into a flowing curve, and pushed firmly into the plastic foam to project out of the cornucopia.

The long trailing pieces are placed in the foam first to create the overall shape; rounder, more solid plant materials follow, filling out the design. To gain the most out of this type of design, the lighter, finer plant materials must be placed to come over the heavier forms, allowing the underlying flowers and leaves to contribute an impression of depth.

PROFESSIONAL TIP

Lead is one of the easiest materials with which to construct containers, but wear gloves if you are going to be handling it a great deal, and wash your hands afterwards.

Basket of Orchard Delights

Fruit is included in this design to create a talking point. Placed in a prominent position near the entrance, the basket would create a welcoming ambiance at a party. Fruits have a natural affinity with flowers and foliage. The combination of flowers and fruit is not new – master painters have combined these two subjects in their works of art since early days – but a constant supply of exotic fruits is now available to the florist. This wonderful range includes fruits such as ornamental pineapples, custard apples, star fruit, cape gooseberries, kiwi fruit, lychee and water melons. Certain vegetables can also provide striking forms for a floral design. These include the globe artichoke (*Cynara scolymus*), sweet corn, peppers, various chillies, red cabbage, sliced in half, and bundles of asparagus.

CHOICE OF MATERIALS

The beautiful rose 'Astra' inspired the colour theme, which was then repeated with furry-textured peaches. A darker, richer shade was added by the plums. Short pieces of *Viburnum davidii* and leather leaf (*Arachniodes adiantiformis)* have been grouped to fill in and add greater variation to the decorative texture. The subtle blue green of the poppies provides a lighter colour contrast. Shredded straw is associated with the packaging of delicate items and is also a good filler material. The bun moss has two uses: it adds a lush green textural quality and covers the posy pad base.

CONTAINER

The large display area within the basket allows the materials to be clearly visible. The rustic weave suggests gardening and

harvesting fruit and vegetables. A posy pad provides a waterproof base to which the fruits, flowers, foliage and moss are secured.

ALTERNATIVE MATERIALS

Arrange strawberries, white roses and small 'White Mountain' lilies in a large glass bowl to give the impression of a dish of strawberries and cream. For a refreshing effect, fill a basket with limes, small grapefruits, lemons, yellow arums and small sunflowers.

CONSTRUCTION METHOD

Assemble the basket, posy pad, crumpled paper, moss, shredded straw, 90mm (20g) wire for hairpins, cocktail sticks, roses, foliage and poppy heads. Lightly soak the posy pad and

Shredded straw and moss hides the mechanics while complementing the peaches and plums.

pack the base of the basket with crumpled paper to support the pad. Place the pad on the paper with its edge resting just below the basket rim. Pack straw around the pad for added security, then hair-pin bun moss and straw to the pad at intervals. Push cocktail sticks into the bases of the peaches and plums, and position them in groups, with larger groups near the centre and smaller ones at the edge. Insert short foliage stems in between the groups of moss, straw and fruits.

Insert roses in groups at various levels, filling any spaces with poppies. Finally, add a trailing hop vine along the handle, gently winding it around the handle with the delicate growing tip entwined into the flowers.

PROFESSIONAL TIP

Alternative containers for this style of design include wooden boxes, and either glass or ceramic bowls; a basket with tall handles, however, is easy to carry and transport.

Harvest Moon

This moon-shaped arrangement is an unusual variant of the traditional upright design, the caging and framing seen in other floristry designs being used on a much larger scale here. As with all large designs, the visual impact begins with the sheer size, and it requires a proportionately spacious setting as a backdrop. Its intricate detailing holds the attention long enough for the soft curves and dramatic colours and shapes of the materials to be fully appreciated. The sharp colouring of the flowers complements the clean simple lines of the wrought-iron stand and the glazed pottery container. The curves and loops of the crescent are perfectly displayed in the tall pedestal. This crescent-style arrangement, with its abundance of fern, is reminiscent of Edwardian splendour and yet the vibrant colouring gives it a very modern up-to-date feel.

CHOICE OF MATERIALS

A delicate tracery of the lace-like fern, *Asparagus setaceus*, is shown to perfection in this design and is an integral part of the arrangement. The wonderfully sensuous curving stems of the arums, *Zantedeschia aethiopica* 'Harvest Moon, complement the loops of the bare-stemmed *Cornus alba* 'Elegantissima'. The lisianthus, *Eustoma russellianum* 'Kyoto Purple', is selected for its strong colour contrast with the arums. The guelder rose (*Viburnum opulus*) echoes the round shape of the design, while glossy *Anthurium andreanum* leaves give visual weight to the centre of the design and contrast with the matt textures of the other materials.

ALTERNATIVE FLOWERS

Asparagus is the ideal foliage; other ferns would change the style of this arrangement. However, in the case of the lilies, the variety 'Mango' could be used, with blue *Trachelium caeruleum* to replace the

eustoma for contrast. A summer choice could be the curving stems of yellow-orange red hot pokers (*Kniphofia*), delicate glory lilies (*Gloriosa roth-schildiana*) and, to give a strong visual impact within the caging, lemon semi-cactus dahlias.

PREPARATION

Fill the container with well-soaked plastic foam; secure it firmly with a mesh of pot tape, and place it in the wrought-iron container. To form the crescent, two curved metal rods, 3–5mm (⅛–¼in) in diameter, are inserted firmly into the foam at each side.

Use small twists of wire covered with paper to secure branches and flowers.

CONSTRUCTION METHOD

The longest stems of cornus can be placed into the foam. To make sure that they curve and loop, they are attached to the metal rods. Once the outline of a frame or cage has been constructed, the foliage and flowers can be woven through. Some of the arum lilies are curved and caught by the cornus stems, which keep them in position. The asparagus fern is inserted into the sides. More is then added so that it flows over the other materials. The rich purple eustoma is evenly distributed throughout the design.

Copper Curves

The elegant straight sides of the coppery gold container inspired this design. The little extra detail of the three rings set into the top right-hand corner of the container gave the idea of incorporating a flexible tube of a similar colour within the design. The tube would give a sense of movement, but at the same time it seemed best to retain the vertical nature of the overall design indicated by the container.

CHOICE OF MATERIALS

A strong central axis is the key to the beauty of this design, and the main flowers were chosen because they had strong vertical stems. The 'Batiste' lily displayed the most suitable habit, with the flower buds curled upright and the open flower heads facing outwards. To strengthen this line, a rose has been included as a secondary flower, accentuating the main axial line of the lilies. The golden peach colour of the rose echoes the soft patina of the metal container.

The patina is also reflected in the micro-bore copper tubing, which is threaded through the design to complement the vertical use of the plant material. Though strong, the metal tubing is flexible and can be bent into soft curves and loops while still retaining its shape. Curving trails of honey-suckle (*Lonicera periclymenum*) echo the curving lines created by the copper tubing.

ALTERNATIVE FLOWERS

A large selection of spring bulbs, including irises and tulips, would be suitable, as would delphiniums, or tall, straight spikes of foxtail lily (*Eremus*), or blazing star (*Liatris*).

The lilies are carefully threaded through the copper swirls and inserted firmly into the foam.

CONSTRUCTION METHOD

The tubing is anchored by threading it through the rings at the front edge of the container; it can then be twisted into a shape to allow the flowers to be added later. The tubing can be further secured by wiring a section and anchoring it into the plastic foam.

When shaping the tubing, hold it against the container at regular intervals and check the effect to make sure that you have a good balance between tighter and more open twists and loops. The plant material is held in place by plastic foam, the tubing providing support for the tall flowers. The tallest is added first and further stems are graded down to create a focal area at the top edge of the container. Softly twisted climbing stems of honeysuckle complete the picture.

PROFESSIONAL TIP

The copper tubing is flexible and will accept the stress of a gradual curve or twist and retain its shape. If tighter curves and spirals are required, the tube may buckle. This can be avoided if the tube is first filled with fine sand, which will take up the strain on the metal. Once the required curve has been achieved, the sand can be poured out very easily.

Classical English Pedestal

This classical design epitomizes the English style of arranging. The triangular outline is filled with a quantity of flowers and foliage types, their stems seeming to radiate from the central focal area. Visual movement results from the repetition of forms, sizes, textures and colours. In contrast with modern or European designs, little space is used within the arrangement, so the eye moves slowly from one flower to the next in a flowing movement. This imposing arrangement should be clearly visible, even to those who are standing, so avoid selecting a low pedestal. A tall one adds height and elegance, but must be stable. This rustic wooden pedestal is complemented by the large basket, and to emphasize the theme, birch branches are twisted and secured around the pedestal and basket.

CHOICE OF MATERIALS

Spike, mass and transitional forms are used in this arrangement. The spike forms establish the outline, the triangular shape being created by bare birch branches, the common foxglove (*Digitalis purpurea*), Solomon's seal (*Polygonatum* x *hybridum*), snowball bush (*Viburnum opulus* 'Sterile') plus yellow arum (*Zantedeschia aethiopica*). *Fatsia japonica* leaves give strength to the outline and add visual depth to the centre.

The mass form of the creamy rose 'Lemon Dream' is used to create a central point of interest. Ranunculus, arums and viburnum flower heads are the transitional forms and fill in the arrangement. A posy of lily of the valley (*Convallaria majalis*) adds a touch of late spring, while fungi are included to add their textured quality and suggest a 'woodland' theme.

To accentuate the woodland theme, bare branches were twisted and secured around the basket.

CONSTRUCTION METHOD

Fill a large dark green plastic bowl with bricks of wet foam and secure them firmly with pot tape. Place the bowl in the basket. Using pot tape, attach green canes to the base of a small plastic container and insert this into the plastic foam; the convallaria will be placed in this container. Firmly insert stems of digitalis, viburnum, Solomon's seal, arum, fatsia leaves and bare branches to establish the height and width of the design.

Add three roses at the centre to create a focal point. Now fill in by placing ranunculus, yellow arums and viburnum stems at various levels. Next, carefully wire the fungi to rest on the edge of the basket. Recess some foliage and flowers to give visual depth; finally, place the bunch of convallaria in its own container.

Lasting Wall Decoration

Artificial flowers combine with dried flowers, natural wood and twigs to produce a design that has tremendous visual impact, even when viewed from a distance. Caged and layered between bleached stems, pale cream lilies and dark brown lotus seed heads offer exciting contrasts between dark and light. Beautifully flowing strands of burgundy *Amaranthus caudatus* soften the strong lines of the bleached twigs and horizontal green leaves. A room with clean, almost stark, lines would be softened by this wall decoration without losing its modern look. This design should be displayed against a pale background to balance the proportions between light and dark colours.

CHOICE OF MATERIALS

Dried flowers can prove difficult resource materials to name accurately. Home-grown dried flowers may be recognizable, but boxes of exotic flowers and seed heads from all over the world can cause problems. Even suppliers will use local names, in particular where the same flower can look very different according to what is left on the stem. Proteas, for example, may have a full flower with all its bracts or simply the base of the flower with no bracts. Some exotics have wonderful names, such as palm fingers, boabub, ata fruits and even elephant grass.

A simple weathered plank and a natural piece of twisted willow (*Salix matsudana* 'Tortuosa') are the basis for the design. Bleached stems, also probably a type of willow, are an integral part of the display, and the lilies were selected to harmonize with the creamy-white stems. To bring out the warm colour of the twisted willow branch, coppery-coloured leaves of hojas, a tropical plant, have been

The amount of space and depth within the caging can be seen here.

selected. Lotus seed heads and fronds of dark brown glycerined fern contrast with the pale colours. Spikes of green leaves, a type of palm, and deep purple palm spears (*Chamaerops humilis*) add further colour to the arrangement. Another woody element is the varnished wood ball, inserted into which are artificial berry bunches. A distinctive softness is added by glycerined love-lies-bleeding (*Amaranthus caudatus*).

ALTERNATIVE MATERIALS

Many other seed pods and dried foliage could be used in this design. The secret is to look closely at the available selection and choose items first for their shape and then the colour. Texture, although important, often develops naturally, as dried materials offer such a range of surface finishes. As a substitute for the lilies, choose any bold artificial flowers that can compete with the scale of the design; the amaranthus could be replaced with glycerined trails of asparagus foliage or chilli peppers threaded on reel wire.

PREPARATION

Secure the twisted willow branch to the plank with plastic-coated garden wire, adding a nail or two where they will not be visible or come through to the back of the wood. The bleached willow is next, forming the outline structure for all the other materials. The stems are tied together with garden wire which is then covered with textured ribbon. The varnished wood ball is attached with the wire and some hot glue.

CONSTRUCTION METHOD

A hot glue gun is essential equipment, as almost all the dried and artificial materials are secured with glue. The hojas leaves and the large-sized lotus seed heads form a framework to which the ferns and the other foliage material can be attached. The shiny dark red berries are attached to the wooden ball by their wire stems. The lilies and the amaranthus complete the design. An interesting feature of this wall display is that particular materials are used at different levels within the design, giving a caged effect.

The Rainforest

Spectacular umbrella leaves set the scene for this miniature rainforest, which can be viewed from all angles. Anthuriums, orchids and some very curious foliage make this a design with some fascinating detail. Shiny aspidistra leaves offer a complete textural contrast to the matt surface of the rather strange-looking burgundy leaves. The abundance of foliage types and varied greens in the design ensures that it has plenty of drama yet is also calming, with a feeling of stability. The foliage, cleverly used as it weaves in and around the flowers, becomes the container in which the other materials are arranged.

CHOICE OF MATERIALS

The exotic-looking umbrella leaves are those of a herbaceous plant, *Darmera peltata* or *Peltiphyllum peltatum*, which has tall pink flowers in the spring. It has completely circular foliage with an attractive edging. The burgundy leaves are *Ligularia dentata* 'Othello'; used at the base of the design, their dark colour contributes a sense of visual stability. *Viburnum rhytidophyllum* has a soft downy fur on the undersides of the leaves and new buds with a lovely veining on the upper side of the foliage. This harmonizes with the small tussocks of bun moss (*Grimmia pulvinata*) that form part of the base of the design. *Aspidistra elatior, Galax urceolata* and the lily grass (*Liriope muscari*) are woven in and out of each other to create an island of foliage which makes an interesting container for the flowers. The bronze orchid hybrid x *Aranda* 'Mohona Gold' is complemented by the soft green of the *Anthurium andreanum* 'Midori'.

The woven container can be clearly seen, with the structural materials forming a design outline.

ALTERNATIVE MATERIALS

Green foliage is essential and any substitutes should look equally tropical. An alternative for the umbrella leaves would be the foliage of the umbrella plant (*Cyperus alternifolius*). A complementary colour harmony could include *Anthurium andreanum* 'Surprise', which is a delicious pink with almost-red veining. The 'Mohona Gold' orchids could be replaced with the green miniature *Cymbidium* 'Malibu'.

PREPARATION

The container for this design is a 35cm (14in) posy pad, a simple plastic container with a disc of plastic foam. When it has been thoroughly soaked, the edge of the foam can be removed or chamfered to soften the edge. The ligularia is prepared by gathering the outer parts of the leaf so that its edges are turned in towards the centre. To keep the leaves in this position, some brightly-coloured wire is caged around each leaf and finally wrapped several times around the neck.

CONSTRUCTION METHOD

Insert the aspidistra leaves into the foam at a sharp angle near the edge of the posy pad. The tip of the leaf is secured with a wire pin. The aspidistra leaves are woven around the edge, with curled galax leaves inserted at intervals. To add to the weaving effect, lily grass is taken over some of the aspidistra leaves. The finished effect gives the impression of a beautifully-woven green container.

Add the viburnum in a strong grouping to one side, with the ligularia visually balancing the leaves towards the centre of the posy pad. In contrast to the normal principles of design, the largest of the umbrella leaves are used to establish the height of the design and the smaller graded to the base, as they grow naturally. The line of anthuriums is then established, with a strong grouping of orchids just off centre. The colourful orchids form a strong focal point amid the cool greens.

Flemish Painting

The great Flemish and Dutch painters of the 17th and 18th centuries created stunning pictures featuring flowers from all seasons in a profusion of beautiful images. They used a full palette of vivid colours, setting a multitude of individual flowers against a dark background. These paintings were for wealthy gardeners and plant collectors, eager to show off a newly-discovered flower or a fantastically-patterned tulip. Often, the flower was more expensive than the painting itself. These masterpieces were a fantasy, conceived from a portfolio of blossoms painted during their seasons. Today's florist is fortunate, with an extensive range of all-year-round materials now available.

CHOICE OF MATERIALS

Spring flowers and shrub materials mix with late summer flowers and even some autumn berries in this design. Painters were also happy to mix together what we nowadays term choice or sophisticated flowers with very ordinary garden or wild flowers, and here we have chosen roses and carnations to complement the sunflower and bluebells.

We have used a host of materials: peonies, roses, rhubarb flowers, delphiniums, sweet peas, bluebells, a sunflower, lilac (*Syringa vulgaris*), foxgloves (*Digitalis purpurea*), marigolds (*Calendula*), day lilies (*Hemerocallis*), Solomon's seal (*Polygonatum*), snowball bush (*Viburnum opulus* 'Sterile'), and a range of foliage types selected to enhance the array of flowers. The arrangement shows how a mixture of varieties and polychromatic colours can create a stunning design that has a kaleidoscope effect.

A mesh or grid of tape is very useful when creating large designs in wide-necked vases.

The design develops from shorter materials at the front and sides which will support longer stems at the back.

PREPARATION

The period of the great Flemish flower paintings covers almost a hundred years, during which time painting techniques developed dramatically. Initially, wooden buckets, jugs and stone containers were used to hold the flowers; later containers were more intricate, including some made from that most technically demanding of materials – glass. The container we have chosen is a terracotta urn, glazed on the inside and with a dusty natural effect on the outside.

Several of the flowers will last better in water rather than plastic foam, so we are using a very practical technique for any wide vase, white tape being fixed to the pot to make a grid that will support the heaviest of flower stems. Clear tape is useful for smaller containers and lighter stems. All the flowers need thorough conditioning beforehand and many of the garden flowers will benefit from the use of a cut flower food.

CONSTRUCTION METHOD

Care must be taken when placing the flowers and foliage in the container to achieve a pleasing visual effect. Balance larger blooms with others that are striking in either colour or shape. Another tip is to group two or three of a dainty flower to counteract the visual weight of larger flowers or leaves. This is a design to enjoy, as materials can easily be moved around without worry. To finish, you may want to add an accessory, such as a bird's nest. Avoid adding insects, however – they are fine in a painting but can cause consternation in the dining room!

One of Life's Pleasures

Receiving a gift of flowers is one of life's pleasures, making any occasion into a special event and one to be remembered. Flowers are the perfect way to express anniversary or birthday greetings, say welcome to a new home or bon-voyage, declare love and affection or simply say a special thank you. The pleasure is increased when the flowers are arranged in an attractive container, and the impact may be further enhanced by the use of exotic and tropical flowers and foliage, which will certainly stimulate much interest because of their unusual shapes and textures.

CHOICE OF MATERIALS

Unusual shapes, plastic-like textures and tropical flowers and foliage are always eye-catching. Here, the important flowers are the orchid, x *Aranda* 'Mohona Gold', and the green *Anthurium andreanum* 'Midori'. The tall bundle of snake grass (*Equisetum*), and New Zealand flax (*Phormium tenax*) provide a strong background for the stems of orchids. Leaves of *Hosta fortunei* 'Aureomarginata' are used to counterbalance the visual weight of the anthuriums and give depth to the base of the design. Trimmed, palm-like leaves of *Cycas revoluta* are balanced on the opposite side by *Alchemilla mollis*, and yellow carnations, *Dianthus* 'Pallas', are grouped together and recessed.

ALTERNATIVE MATERIALS

Either dogwood (*Cornus alba*), or contorted willow (*Salix matsudana* 'Tortuosa'), could be used to give the height needed. For a more exotic touch, use small proteas, helianthus, sunflowers, strelitzias or 'Mango' arums, combined with comparably bold foliage, such as aspidistra, *Fatsia japonica* or *Calathea makoyana*.

CONTAINER

Tall and simple, this yellow ceramic container is an integral part of the arrangement, as it adds height and creates a visual balance with the bold, clear groups of the flowers and foliage. It also provides a subtle colour link with the recessed carnations. The container is intended as a lovely and permanent gift in its own right, for once the current arrangement has faded it can easily be refilled with a different combination of flowers and foliage.

CONSTRUCTION METHOD

Condition all flowers and foliage. Pre-soak foam in a flower food solution, then secure it into the container. Create height with snake grass and New Zealand flax; add the orchid stems, and give width and depth with palm and hosta leaves. Strengthen the outline with two anthuriums. Use a support wire to position a bundle of snake grass at the base of the hosta leaves in the centre. Fill in the sides with alchemilla; recess short-stemmed carnations in a group. Finally, insert the third anthurium just above the snake grass bundle.

Use bold groups of foliage and orchids to establish the height. Palm and hosta leaves create the width and depth.

PROFESSIONAL TIP

To make the snake grass bundle, cut grass into 15cm (6in) lengths. Group them and tie firmly with some raffia. An additional touch that will be appreciated by the recipient would be to enclose a card giving the plant names and countries of origin.

Mother's Day Delights

Mother's Day poses the perennial problem of selecting the right gift for mother on her special day. There are many tempting presents to choose from, such as perfume, books or chocolates, but the florist has more to offer. This includes a delightful selection of cut flowers and foliage designs and flowering pot plants, at a range of prices to suit every purse. For a small child, or for someone on a tight budget, the ideal gift might be a basket of polyanthus or saintpaulias, or perhaps miniature daffodils, whereas planted bowls, and large handtieds or arrangements are lovely presents from someone with no financial restraints. However, the following arrangements are for mums who prefer something different, adore beautiful flowers and appreciate innovative and exciting design ideas incorporating new structures.

FLORAL SURPRISE

CHOICE OF MATERIALS

For this wooden box arrangement, the emphasis is on femininity. Delicate forms and textures of flowers and foliage are combined with subtle pastel pinks, creams and pale greens. The creamy white lily, 'Sterling Star', pink roses and strap-shaped leaves of the iris are used in strong vertical placements. These are counter-balanced by gently curving lines of tulips and twisting stems of honeysuckle (sp. *Lonicera japonica*). To create immediate impact, stems of dainty lily of the valley (*Convallaria majalis*) are bunched and placed on two different levels. The filigree effect of the single lilac, *Syringa microphylla* 'Superba' repeats the dainty form of the convallaria. Fresh green moss, nestled between the slats of the box, gives an attractive finish to the arrangement.

ALTERNATIVE MATERIALS

A wide range of beautiful and attractive flowers could be used, including stems of *Prunus triloba*, orchids such as *Oncidium* 'Golden Shower' or *Aranthera* 'James Storey', gerberas, ranunculus, eustoma, bouvardia or spray roses.

CONTAINER

The natural wood of the box containers is most appealing. Two boxes, one of medium size and the other small, have been glued firmly together. This creates a variation of height, allowing two placements of flowers and foliage.

CONSTRUCTION METHOD

Line one medium box and one small box with black polythene. Place the small box on the top of medium box, positioning it to one side and towards the back, and glue firmly in position. To hide any visible black polythene, glue moss between the wooden slats. Secure foam into both boxes.

Establish the height and create the structure by inserting lilies, roses, freesias and iris leaves in parallel groupings, intertwining these groups with the twisting stems of the honeysuckle. Insert the curving stems of the lilac and honeysuckle at the outer edges. Place the tulips in a gently curving line to give visual weight; add two aspidistra leaves to the back, and one syngonium leaf to the side in the lower arrangement. Now group the lily of the vally together in the centre of the small box and to the side in the lower box. Hairpin moss into position to cover any visible foam.

PROFESSIONAL TIP

This arrangement requires the flowers and foliage
to be used in positive groupings and rhythmic
lines. If convallaria were used singly, the stems
would look insignificant. Create maximum impact
by gathering many stems with their natural
foliage; arrange them into a posy, secured with
an elastic band, and place them in the design.

ROCOCO BOWL

CHOICE OF MATERIALS

The inspiration for this arrangement was the lovely tulip 'Park Rococo', for its delicate apricot, soft green streaks and slight mauve tinge made it irresistible. The freesia was chosen to intensify the mauve colouring and provide a contrast, while the foliage echoes the green markings on the tulips and the 'Safari' roses strengthen the apricot colouring. The tulips' pliable stems and the trails of *Asparagus setaceus* are easy to thread through the cage structure. The loops of bear grass (*Xerophyllum tenax*), and gold wire are added to repeat the caged feeling.

CONTAINER

The traditional ceramic bowl, has been chosen as its apricot colour will both echo and enhance the colours of the flowers. Another factor is that the solid bowl is stable and capable of holding foam, the cage structure, a quantity of flowers and foliage, and water.

CONSTRUCTION METHOD

Make a simple elongated structure from 30cm (12in) lengths of willow, secured together with 0.56mm (24g) wire. To give a neat finish, cover the wire with raffia. Secure plastic foam into the bowl with pot tape and place the cage structure over the foam. The structure is secured with plastic-coated wire, which is then inserted into the foam.

Starting at the outside edges of the structure, weave the tulip stems and trailing pieces of *Asparagus setaceus* into the centre. Add stems of freesia between the tulips, and then recess some roses and more asparagus.

The finishing touch is added by weaving gold-coloured wire through the structure, and then taking loops of bear grass over the top of the design and securing both ends either to the foam or the cage structure.

PROFESSIONAL TIP

When making the structure, only use stems which are pliable and easy to manipulate. Make the willow cage structure well in advance and store until required.

Sympathy designs

Memorable tributes

Whether it be a complex and elaborate design or a single flower, every sympathy tribute is an individual and unique mark of respect. Funeral customs have their origin in an ancient need for ritual, and have always been a gentle mark of sorrow, but at the same time, the following designs represent a departure from conventional funeral tributes, with 'designer' touches that make them refreshing and memorable.

EFFICIENT SERVICE

One of the florist's important jobs – and this applies equally to a close friend who may feel the need to prepare a tribute with a personal touch – is to ensure that a sympathy flowers service runs smoothly and with professionalism. The information gathered from the customer must be checked for accuracy, which may mean following up a request for flowers by looking for the obituary in the local paper or conferring with the funeral director. Names, dates, addresses and, most essentially, times are extremely important.

With these details firmly established, a tribute can be designed to the customer's specifications, while bearing several factors in mind. Main tributes, usually from the immediate family, are carried on top of the coffin. Modern hearses have very little roof space, and it is worth dicussing larger designs with the funeral director. When several tributes are sent, extra cars are used for flowers. Pay attention to minor details: ensure that designs are well drained and will not drip; remove lily stamens that can mark a cuff or gloves; check that cards are firmly attached and clearly written and, finally, ensure that drivers are appropriately dressed and do not leave the radio blaring when making a delivery either to the funeral director or to the home.

FRAMES

The plastic foam frames that are now used for most tributes have brought about a major change in the way sympathy designs are produced. Frames are available in the full range of traditional shapes as well as numbers, letters and recent introductions, such as angels and trains. Manufacturers continue to improve the range, and are now introducing new biodegradable frames, designed to avoid harming the environment.

Plastic foam frames are easier and cleaner to use than the traditional wire frames padded with sphagnum moss. Compared with the skills required for success with wire and moss frames, the techniques needed to make tributes with foam frames are far more speedily and simply acquired. Flowers last longer in the wet foam; professionals find that their work patterns and schedules need not be as frantic as in the past, and in addition to these advantages, the wet foam frames give designers – professional and amateur alike – a greater ability to be innovative and creative with combinations of materials, colours and textures.

The use of sphagnum moss and wire frames has not entirely disappeared, however, and many holly wreaths are used as memorial designs at Christmas or as designs to be placed on a door. The trend in some European countries is to return to the traditional moss-covered frames because of the natural qualities inherent in the living material. It is clear that today's florist needs a broad range of practical skills.

An intricate and sensitive detailing of sympathy designs displays the creative skills of the designer.

LEFT The use of grouping and overbinding add movement and interest to this swirling cluster wreath.

BELOW The European funeral spray uses flowers carefully arranged so that they appear to be artlessly growing in natural groups as if in a cottage garden.

PERSONALIZED TRIBUTES

Flowers are often the last gift from the living to a loved one, and customers frequently request specific and perhaps unusual tributes. These may reflect an aspect of the deceased's lifestyle or character. To this end, the florist will discreetly ask questions about interests, hobbies, favourite flowers and colours. Florists often need considerable personal qualities to deal with bereaved families and friends. They must be fully aware that the tributes serve almost a healing purpose, and flowers may become the focus for conversation.

In addition to preformed foam shapes, there are now designer sheets. These have a polystyrene-type base and plastic foam upper layer and can be cut into unusual shapes. Another valuable aid is the designer block. A large square block of plastic foam, it can be sculpted into three-dimensional designs. As templates cannot always be used, a steady hand is required.

SYMPATHY DESIGNS

The vast range of possibilites and the influence of modern trends in floristry can be seen in the designs that follow. The natural and ecological movement is reflected in the European sympathy spray, in which the flowers appear to be growing in natural groups.

The woven cushion also reflects the trend towards the natural way of arranging, but at the same time the cushion, thistle and pillow designs echo the Victorian need to represent everyday items in flowers. The skills used in the three-dimensional Scottish thistle have applications in other areas, such as flower floats and displays. The fleur de lys emblem evokes pagan well dressing, though in recent years the technique of setting individual petals and leaves into moist clay has been much used to depict biblical scenes. It is also particularly useful when creating business or sporting logos for special functions or events.

Sympathy tributes have moved on from the days of moss and wire, not simply to include plastic foam, but also glue, and a sophisticated use of cut materials from all over the world. Grouping, weaving and overbinding are all terms in current usage when developing contemporary funeral designs.

Floral Casket

Created for a funeral service, this very lovely informal style of tribute has tremendous appeal, forming a blanket of flowers that can cover the casket completely. The design can be a main tribute from family or a smaller version can be made as a general tribute. Here, the deep rich colours of the tree peonies are enhanced by the pale lilies and the flushed pinks and mauves of the roses and carnations, the flowers and foliage being placed in groups to emphasize and strengthen their visual impact. The size and proportions of the tribute are versatile and can be adjusted to suit the individual requirements.

CHOICE OF MATERIALS

The glowing colours of the carnation, *Dianthus* 'Charmeur', and blossom of the crab apple, *Malus* 'Profusion', inspired this tribute. Pale green *Nephrolepis exaltata* fern, ruscus, glossy aspidistra, foxtail fern (*Asparagus meyeri*), the strap leaves of typha, bold bergenia leaves and *Viburnum* x *bodnantense* were to contribute to the strong foliage outline of this design.

The flowers had to achieve a balance of boldness and strength through either colour or form. The creamy white lily 'Sterling Star', 'Valerie' roses and the glorious deep crimson tree peonies, *Paeonia suffruticosa*, were used to strengthen the rich colouring of this design.

ALTERNATIVE FLOWERS

You might consider designs made with one type of flower, such as a single colour of rose or lily. Perhaps subtle blends of colours of one type of flower, such as sweet peas or tulips, could also be effective, or even a smaller design with a mixture of fragrant freesias.

PREPARATION

The foundation, consisting of a large block of foam encased in a plastic cage with a handle, needs to be thoroughly soaked in water and all the flower and foliage material must be conditioned before use. The tree peonies and malus blossom will benefit if warm, rather than cold, water is used.

CONSTRUCTION METHOD

The length and width of this symmetrical diamond-shaped design is established with the foliage and malus blossom. The foliage is placed firmly into the foam in groups, with the nephrolepis fern taken across the foam in a line. As well as being such an integral part of the design the foliage helps to give protection to the more delicate flowers.

The longer stems of carnations and roses are placed into the foam. Use the bars of the plastic cage to support the stems of the longer flowers. The focal or accent flowers, two roses and two stems of recessed lilies, are used to establish the focal area and height of the design. The length and focal area can then be joined using the medium and shorter length flowers. All stem ends need to be cut with a diagonal cut or point to ensure correct insertion and hold in the foam. To link with the grouped foliage, the roses and carnations are also grouped, in pairs, throughout the design.

For the most part, the foliage is used at the outer edge of the foam, allowing plenty of space for the flowers.

The Eternal Circle

The wreath is the most traditional of all the funeral tributes, the first known examples being wreaths over 3,000 years old, found in the tombs of the Egyptian Pharaohs. These were made from herbs, sweet-smelling flowers and grasses, all bound together to make a ring, the shape representing the eternal circle. Since the first quarter of this century, florists have been making wreaths on circular wire frames bound with either straw or moss, the flowers being wired individually and pushed into the base frame. Pre-formed shapes and sizes of ring have now become readily available, allowing strong-stemmed flowers to be pushed into the foam without wiring, so reducing the time taken to make a wreath. With some adaptation of these pre-formed frames, individuality can still be achieved.

CHOICE OF MATERIALS

All designs have a starting point or trigger; this design started with the selection of the beautiful king proteas. How could these be used to maximum effect? The leaves of *Leucadendron argentea* are as lovely as the clear pink bracts of the protea. The idea was to layer the shapes one on top of the other in a fish-scale fashion, shading from the brightest pink to the palest green. The centres of the proteas have an architectural feel and were to be used as the dominant focus for the design. To intensify the colour of the pink bracts and to enhance the exotic selection suggested by the proteas, orchids – in this case *Aranthera* 'James Storey' – were also included. The plant selection was finished with the choice of rich reddish rhubarb stems, to be used in a twisted stem effect, completing the wreath shape.

To make the design even more interesting, it was decided to cut away a quarter of the pre-form foam base. The gap could then be joined in an open pattern by rhubarb stems.

ALTERNATIVE FLOWERS

Many types of leaves can be used to give the layered scale look and these will last for a while. For a very beautiful if short-lived effect, petals from flowers such as tulips, roses and lilies can also be used. A range of fleshy-stemmed herbaceous plants could be adapted to achieve the same effect as the rhubarb.

CONSTRUCTION METHOD

Cut a quarter out of a pre-formed foam-based wreath frame. The frame will weaken but can be strengthened by completing the circle with a metal rod, 3mm (⅛in) gauge. The pink bracts and silver leaves are removed and attached to the frame by a piece of wire shaped like a hairpin; this is then covered by the next layer of leaves or bracts. The rhubarb stems are trimmed slightly longer than the cut-away quarter and wires are pushed into the ends. These are then pushed into the foam base and the orchids are woven through to add interest, colour and texture.

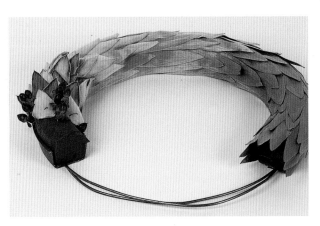

The foam on each side of the cut ring is filled with flowers, foliage and, finally, the rhubarb stems.

PROFESSIONAL TIP

Time needs to be taken to strengthen the base frame. The layering of the bracts and leaves is also worth taking time over to give an even and professional look. The rhubarb will be easier to use if allowed to go slightly soft before bending; once in the foam and taking up water it will become firm again.

Textured Pillow

M any of the traditional sympathy tributes have symbolic qualities associated with their shape. The cross, for example, is the sign of Christianity, while a heart is a token of great love and affection. The chaplet denotes sportsmanship or military honour, and the pillow represents peaceful sleep. In this particular pillow design, great emphasis is placed on the selection of materials, which should have a visually soft textural quality, yet distinctive shape. They are placed in groups which vary in size and shape, and are used to establish height, form pathways or create individual areas of interest within the overall effect.

CHOICE OF MATERIALS

The soft green mass of the bun moss is placed on the tribute to create visual movement across the base. The soft curving lines of the tulip 'Queen of the Night' repeat this rhythmic pattern. The full-petalled rose 'Delilah' adds visual height. Pools of green hellebores (*Helleborus lividis*) and the flowers of the snowball bush (*Viburnum opulus* 'Roseum') merge with the moss and roses; the cream-coloured foliage of *Pieris formosa* 'Forrestii' adds a vibrant touch of colour. The subtle softness is provided by short stems of the herb purple sage, while the outline shape is created by a mixture of foliage, including *Galax urceolata* leaves, leather leaf (*Arachniodes adiantiformis*), and ming fern (*Asparagus umbellatus*), which gently integrate with the other groupings. Extra interest is added by the stems of the small allium flowers, which are wired internally allowing them to twist over the moss.

ALTERNATIVE MATERIALS

Lilies and mini-gerberas would be attractive alternatives to the roses and tulips. Hydrangeas could replace the viburnum and double lisianthus (*Eustoma russellianum*) could be substituted for the hellebores.The bun moss and mixed foliage are the main feature of this particular design, and anything substituted for these would entail the loss of their important textural qualities and their soft, gentle appearance.

CONSTRUCTION METHOD

Pre-soak the foam-based frame, and gather together the various types of foliage, flowers, moss and wires. The flowers and foliage, particularly the pieris, need to be well conditioned before use. Establish the distinctive pillow shape by grouping the different foliage types. Ensure that the corners are pointed and clearly defined. Position the bun moss to create a pathway across the frame and then hairpin it firmly in place. Insert the tulips, following the line of the moss. Group roses together to create the overall height, then place the remaining roses on different levels, inserting several of those with short-stems low down on the base. Now add the groups of green hellebores, viburnum flowers, and pieris foliage. Finally insert a 0.56mm (24g) stub wire into each hollow allium stem; form it into a gentle curve, and insert it in the foam base, carefully arching the stem over the moss. Lightly spray the finished pillow with water, and store in a cool place. Just before delivery, add the card.

PROFESSIONAL TIP

Many people are confused as to the difference between a pillow and a cushion. Simply, the latter is square, while the pillow has a natural, elongated shape with gently curving indentations and well-defined corner points. A pleated ribbon or single leaf edging would be too precise for this design, so groupings of foliage are used for a natural finish.

Fleur de Lys

Florists are often called upon to imitate real-life objects in flowers and foliage. A type of sympathy tribute that can take a considerable amount of thought and time is the emblem or logo. Emblems have been used since medieval times to identify groups of people. In those days, the coat of arms, or heraldic device, was used to enable men to identify each other in battle. Today, crests, emblems or logos are used to identify organizations, institutions, societies or businesses. A *fleur de lys* pattern on a church floor tile became the inspiration for this design.

CHOICE OF MATERIALS

Many flower and foliage materials can be used for two-dimensional images of this type. Intricate symbols require individual leaves or even petals. For this design, it was appropriate to use a selection consisting entirely of foliage. The leaves of *Eleagnus* x *ebbengii* have two distinct colours: the underside is a very good silver cream that made it an ideal choice for the *fleur de lys* symbol and, conveniently, the topside is a deep dark green that would be excellent to represent the background of the tile. Bear grass (*Xerophyllum tenax*) and iris leaves completed the selection. Gold-coloured wire added distinction to the finished design.

PREPARATION

As the foliage is received, it will benefit from being well conditioned before use. In the meantime, the foundation for the design – a designer sheet – can be prepared. This is a board consisting of a top layer of normal plastic foam with a harder and more solid base beneath. The base is still lightweight, and can be cut with a knife, but is strong enough to take a fair amount of weight when fully soaked. Designer board is supplied in varying sizes, but is generally rectangular in shape, and in this case the board needs to be trimmed into a square. When conditioned, the individual leaves are cut from the branches and graded.

ALTERNATIVE MATERIALS

Reindeer moss is available in many different colours and is a useful material for marking out shapes, as are carnations and carnation sprays. Other suitable foliage includes laurel, acuba and camellia. A strong contrast in texture and colour between image and background will ensure that the logo has a sharp outline.

Top quality eleagnus leaves are used to complete the symbol before the background is filled in.

PROFESSIONAL TIP

Use photocopies of the symbol, perhaps taken from a letter heading, to make a template. The photocopies can be blown up or reduced until they are the appropriate size for the design. The template can then be used to mark out the pattern on the designer sheet. Use a pin or sharp pencil to punch holes through the template. Always make sure you have researched or been given all the information required.

CONSTRUCTION METHOD

The designer sheet is lightly soaked. It is helpful to use a template to mark out the pattern in the plastic foam. The leaves for the *fleur de lys* are pinned to the foam either with wire pins made from stub wire or with manufactured pins. The tip of each leaf will mask the pin that secured its predecessor. The smaller leaves are used for the three points, building up to bigger leaves in the centre and at the base. The background leaves are then pinned to the base with the edges tucked under the silver leaves to keep the distinctive shape sharp and clear. To conceal the final row of pins and to give a professional finish, the strap-shaped leaves of the iris are secured neatly around the edge of the frame. The bear grass and the gold-coloured wire are inserted firmly at the base of the *fleur de lys*, in between the eleagnus leaves. Gold wire is used to bind the strands of bear grass and wire attractively together at the points, and the two wire ends are inserted firmly into the foam through the foliage.

Thoughts of a Spring Meadow

European designer florists use groups of flowers, foliage, plants, stems, branches and moss as they are seen in their natural surroundings as a source of inspiration. This natural style of design can successfully be applied to a range of funeral tributes, and in particular to the sympathy spray. With its garden-like appearance, it appeals to those who request a less formal tribute. The effect is achieved by placing flowers, foliage and branches at different heights and on various levels in clear, easily seen groups. The base finish is an important feature of the design: the technique is to build up an attractive covering by using definite groupings of single leaves, branches, stems of flowers and varied foliage, all linked together by fresh moss to produce a textured finish.

CHOICE OF MATERIALS

The selection, which reflects a spring garden, includes drumstick primulas, 'Golden Apeldoorn' tulips, 'Blue Moon' freesias, 'Blue Magic' irises, *Narcissus* 'Carlton' and also a miniature daffodil, a polyanthus plant, a variety of golden conifer, *Gaultheria shallon,* common box (*Buxus sempervirens*), and rhododendron. Twisted wisteria branches add interest and fresh sphagnum moss conceals the foam base and the polyanthus root ball.

ALTERNATIVE MATERIALS

Select materials which have seasonal and garden associations. A summer design, for example, might include such traditional garden favourites as larkspur, roses, lilies, scabious, sweetpeas and wheat.

BASE

Here, a specially-designed base called a Raquette is used, but two bricks of foam firmly secured into a long plastic tray would also be suitable. A large area of foam is required at the base to support the wide range of plant materials.

LEFT Knock the polyanthus from its pot, remove surplus soil and make a round root ball. Cover this with poly-thene and secure with twine.

BELOW Add the materials at different levels.

CONSTRUCTION METHOD

Cover the prepared root ball with sphagnum moss, attaching this with wire. Using 1.25mm (18g) wire, secure the polyanthus to the base.

Establish the height of the spray with a group of iris leaves, long-stemmed daffodils, primulas and iris stems; now add width and soften the edges with groups of various foliage types and short-stemmed flowers. Intertwine branches of wisteria and hair-pin clumps of moss into position. Complete the groupings by placing more primulas, irises and daffodils on different levels. Add miniature daffodils to the centre. Check that the base foam is attractively concealed with groups of leaves or moss.

PROFESSIONAL TIP

Moss is an important feature of the design, as it provides a link between the groupings of flowers and foliage, as well as covering the foam base and adding a natural finish to the textured base.

Scottish Thistle

The skills and expertise used in the designing and making of sympathy tributes can be transferred into other areas. This amusing, almost cartoon style of design, primarily made as a sympathy tribute, could equally be used as a centrepiece for a Hogmanay party or perhaps for a birthday party with a Scottish theme. The national flower of the Scots is used as a logo on many products originating in Scotland, but the simple beauty of the flower is often overlooked, perhaps because of the sharpness of its prickly foliage.

CHOICE OF MATERIALS

Liatris spicata 'Blue Bird' was an obvious choice. Its colour and its effectiveness when the flower spikes are grouped together made it ideal for this design. Several varieties of silver foliage could have been used for the almost-scaly base of the thistle, but *Senecio* 'Sunshine' was selected. The dramatic foliage at the sides of the thistle is actually from the globe artichoke plant (*Cynara cardunculus* or cardoon), the flowers of which resemble a giant thistle. The moss at the base is complemented by the dark green ivy, *Hedera helix*. These plant materials give a suggestion of the highland glens where the thistle can be found in abundance.

ALTERNATIVE FLOWERS

There are several types of foliage that could be used instead of the senecio. The reverse silver side of *Eleagnus* x *ebbingei* or the pointed silver leaf of *Leucadendron argenteum* are two good examples. The flowers for the thistle could be represented with purple statice (*Limonium*). In the spring, lilac would be a good choice.

PREPARATION

A posy pad is used as the base for the design and blocks of plastic foam are used for the thistle. The plastic foam is first shaped carefully with a knife; then a hot-melt glue gun can be used to fix it securely to the base. For extra security, slim plant canes around 10cm (4in) in length are inserted in the posy pad and the plastic foam is speared onto them. After a few minutes, the glue will be set and the foam can then be gently soaked with water.

The senecio leaves are stripped from the main stem, any damaged leaves discarded, and the remainder are graded into different sizes. All the materials must be thoroughly conditioned as there will be only a limited water reservoir for the fresh materials.

ABOVE The completed cup shape of the thistle can clearly be seen.

RIGHT Begin by inserting the liatris at the centre, turning the design frequently to ensure that it looks balanced from all angles.

CONSTRUCTION METHOD

To begin the design, the smallest senecio leaves are pinned to the upper edge of the base. The pins are made with 0.70mm (22g) gauge stub wire; alternatively, pre-made florists' pins can be used. The next row of leaves will hide the pins. As each row of senecio is added, the leaves gradually increase in size, until the largest leaves are at the base of the thistle. To hide the last row of pins, and as a decorative feature, small bunches of senecio buds are inserted into the posy pad. The moss used on the base of the design does not on its own give sufficient visual weight to the base of the arrangement and the addition of ivy leaves provides an easy and attractive solution to the problem. For extra versatility and security, they can be loop-stitched with a 0.36mm (28g) silver or green annealed wire.

The liatris can then be grouped together fairly tightly at the centre of the senecio leaves. The colourful flower spikes come right to the edge of the senecio. The dramatic artichoke leaves contribute a final flourish to the centrepiece.

PROFESSIONAL TIP

Many real-life objects can be successfully represented in a three-dimensional design made with flowers. Research your chosen subject well, making sketches and drawings before you start the design itself. It is important to keep the outline as simple as possible, as complicated shapes are not always easy to work with. Allow for the depth of the chosen flowers or foliage when constructing the framework.

Swirling Cluster Wreath

The traditional wreath is given a novel twist here. The swirling motion of the flower and foliage groupings contributes a strong visual rhythm. Plenty of detail gives the design even more visual interest, which is further emphasized by the loops of bear grass that are taken over the clusters of flowers, foliage and bun moss. The gold, creams and blues are offset with greens that range from the almost black aspidistra leaves to the palest green-white of the guelder rose and lily of the valley.

CHOICE OF MATERIALS

The flowers and foliage types are grouped together fairly tightly, and it is therefore important to make sure that there are plenty of contrasts in shape, colour and texture. The three main groupings of flowers are 'Limona' roses, lily of the valley (*Convallaria majalis*), and Persian buttercup (*Ranunculus asiaticus*). The crisp white spikes of the lily of the valley are a good foil for the more rounded and warmer colours of the roses and ranunculus.

Other choices for the smaller clusters are rich blue hydrangeas, lime-green *Helleborus corsicus*, the creamy green guelder rose (*Viburnum opulus*) and a host of foliage types. Leather leaf (*Arachniodes adianti-formis*) and *Aspidistra elatior* are similar in that both are glossy, but there the similarity ends: the leather leaf is dainty and lace-like, while the aspidistra is bold and solid. The smaller-leafed foliage types include hebe, euonymus, skimmia, myrtle, yew and the rounded leaf of *Galax urceolata*.

Groupings can be completed on one side of the wreath before starting a new cluster on the other side.

ALTERNATIVE FLOWERS

In autumn, as an alternative to the traditional reds and oranges, try purple asters or michaelmas daisies, lime-green spider chrysanthemums, purple phlox and bright orange Chinese lanterns (*Physalis alkekengi franchetii*). The foliage should include the dark, almost black leaves of purple beech (*Fagus sylvatica*).

PREPARATION

The foam frame is thoroughly soaked with tepid water containing cut flower food. Ranunculus does not always thrive in plastic foam, and the food seems to counteract its adverse effects. Once soaked, the inner and outer corners of the foam can be chamfered. This makes the foam easier to work with and to hide.

CONSTRUCTION METHOD

The cut materials are laid out on the bench in roughly the order in which they will be placed in the foam. This provides an opportunity to alter and re-arrange some of

the flowers and foliage so that different textures and shapes are adjacent to each other. Starting with one of the main groupings, the materials can be inserted into the frame. Some of the flowers and the foliage will need to be secured tightly with wire pins. The shapes of the clusters should be angled to look as if they are moving around the frame. To complete the wreath, loops of bear grass (*Xerophyllum tenax*) are attached, using stub wires for extra security. To add a distinctive touch, one loop of the grass is replaced by flowering

spikes of *Heuchera* 'Jubilee'. The soft pink and yellowy green harmonize beautifully with the gentle flush of the 'Limona' roses.

PROFESSIONAL TIP

A knife or pointed stem end is used to mark out on the plastic foam the three main areas for the flowers. This helps to ensure that the roses, lily of the valley and ranunculus are spaced evenly apart. You might also mark out an indication of the shape the flowers are to fill.

Woven Beauty

The modern trend towards selecting flowers for their natural form is now starting to affect sympathy floristry, allowing the progressive florist to create a design in tune with the innate beauty of the flowers and foliage. Wild materials, chosen for their structural and textural properties and rich earthiness, provided the starting point for this sympathy tribute, giving a modern and natural look to the traditional shape of the design. In fact, the selection of materials seen here could be used not only for sympathy work but for any type of arrangement, as the plant materials have been chosen for their individual qualities, the flowing stems contributing to the finished piece.

CHOICE OF MATERIALS

The decision was made to create an overall finished look that was open and had a great deal of visual depth and texture. When stripped of its leaves, birch can be used to create a fine open tracery of branches and twigs, and the dark colour of the stems helps to create depth when combined with bright and vibrant colours. The arums (*Zantedeschia aethiopica*) have soft and pliable stems which add interest to the tracery of stems in the design as a whole. The rich orange of the variety 'Mango' gives highlights of colour and intensifies the orange in the *Cryptomeria japonica*, which was chosen for its dense but feathery texture, adding further depth and visual weight.

ALTERNATIVE FLOWERS

Many shrubs and trees can be used to create the framework, but it is essential that the stems are strong and flexible – willows and alder have these qualities. The flowers should have pliable stems, such as those of tulips or muscari.

Foam in a plastic cage is securely attached to an outer corner of the cushion by threading stub wires through the frame of garden wire.

CONSTRUCTION METHOD

The outline shape is formed from four pieces of strong garden wire, each about 45cm (18in) in length. These are bent into shallow curves and the ends are bound together with florists' wire to create an overall cushion shape. Cross pieces of birch stem are then added to strengthen the wire outline. Bear in mind that this is only a framework to which other plant materials will be added, and remember that the finished piece must be sufficiently strong to allow it to be picked up and moved several times.

The remaining birch twigs are woven to create an open tracery, which can be secured with fine wire if necessary. Either a piece of plastic foam covered with wire mesh or a pre-made framed foam base is added. This is secured within the branches to hold the arum stems and will later be covered by cryptomeria.

One by one, each arum stem is threaded through at the point where the head will finally be positioned, the stems being eased through until pushed into the foam pad. The cryptomeria then completes the design.

PROFESSIONAL TIP
The twigs need to be sufficiently strong to act as a frame or skeleton to allow other soft-stemmed materials to be woven through them, creating a flowing and interesting pattern of stems, leaves and flowers.

Floral weddings

Creative inspiration

Brides are generally romantics at heart, at least when it comes to this very special occasion. Many, while not understanding a great deal about flowers, will be aware of the effect they can create and appreciate their importance in creating the ideal atmosphere for the wedding. Modern couples can choose to hold their weddings in a wide range of venues, and such diverse settings as a country estate or a football club will often provide the inspiration for a creative and unusual theme for the wedding.

Beautiful wedding flowers can reflect the personality of the bride, and help to create a joyful atmosphere.

THE CHOICES AVAILABLE

In this chapter you will find bouquets that emphasize the importance of selecting flowers for their colour, form and textural impact. Most varieties are available all year round and you will be able to assist the bride to choose the flowers of her dreams, as well as make the most effective use of good design principles.

Even with the staggering availability of flowers, a choice that reflects the season of a particular wedding can add great charm to the bride's bouquet. In fact the simplicity and beauty of the natural materials are all-important ingredients in the success of the overall effect. The Winter Wedding bouquet combines the rich colouring and natural beauty of parrot tulips with the twisted effect of trailing stems, creating a wonderfully open and wild-looking bouquet.

TECHNIQUES AND SKILLS

Designs have also been chosen to show the range of techniques used in modern floristry, from classic bouquets carried over the arm to modern handtied and spiralled designs. The Lilac and Lilies design, made with white lilac and arum lilies, creates a flowing cascade to delight any bride. The complementary Spring Posy develops the theme, adding other flowers to those of the bride to create an overall impression of the clear, fresh colours of spring. This contrasts with the Summer design, which is a classic waterfall bouquet, beautifully executed with a breath-taking range of delicate summer flowers in soft pastels.

Wedding flowers need to be at their peak for just one day, but even so this is too long for some materials to survive and remain fresh without water. New ideas and techniques enable us to use wet foam holders for delicate flowers, such as sweet peas, that easily wilt.

There are many ideas in these pages for creative solutions and a fresh insight into possible wedding designs.

FLOWERS AND FABRICS

The bride's and the bridesmaids' dresses are usually the crucial elements in establishing the theme for the whole event and this is reflected in the great care taken to choose them. The style, fabrics and colours of the gowns will initially suggest the colour scheme for the wedding and choices for the floral designs. A billowing romantic dress with full train and veil will look stunning with a loose, flowing waterfall style of bouquet, whereas a short or straight-skirted dress will be seen to greater advantage with a posy or tighter bouquet. Nowadays, not all wedding dresses are white, and the more colourful and unusual fabrics can inspire exciting textured bouquets.

Experienced florists are able to use a broad range of unusual flowers, berries, fruits, and even vegetables. On the left, elderberries and ribbons create an impression of autumnal abundance, while below, passion flowers and artichokes are used in a distinctive combination with lilies and roses.

THE PERFECT BOUQUET

An interview with the bride will help to build up an understanding of her personality and assist you in creating the ideal design for her. She will have had a vision of her bouquet in mind for a long time, and a sensitive florist will use his or her expertise to help direct and complete this picture. The aim is to create a design that interprets the bride's wishes, and enhances and brings out her personality, rather than over-whelming her. Professional florists know from years of experience that the fulfilment of the bride's ideas and the initial pleasure on her face as she sees the bouquet is a most rewarding moment for a floral designer.

Cascade of Lilac and Lilies

After the cold austerity of the winter months, spring brings a bounty of colour, scents and textures. This spring-time tied bouquet, designed to be carried over the bride's arm, is the epitome of the new season's abundance. The tied overarm or informal presentation bouquet is not a new type of design. Many Edwardian brides carried tied bouquets, and the overarm bouquet was again popular in the 1920s. In the late 1990s, this cascading tied design is increasingly popular with brides-to-be and with florists.

CHOICE OF MATERIALS

Fragrant lilac (*Syringa vulgaris*) is combined with waxy arum or calla lilies (*Zantedeschia aethiopica*). Both are complemented by the filigree fern *Asparagus setaceus*, the small flowers of *Exochorda* x *macrantha* 'The Bride' and the ivory colour of the freesia 'Elegance'

ALTERNATIVE FLOWERS

The overarm bouquet can be designed with a myriad of other flowers and foliage types for different times of the year. As an alternative choice of flowers for the spring, for example, the readily-available purple lilac could be used with lemon-yellow arum lilies. Lilac, freesia and creamy scented narcissi could complete the bouquet. The combination of the purples and yellows would make a dramatic springtime statement.

PREPARATION

All materials need to be well conditioned, especially the woody shrub, exochorda. This delicate blossom is well behaved when picked with just the bottom florets open.

CONSTRUCTION METHOD

Start the bouquet with a lily and some of the shorter lilac. The design is built around this first placement, the longer stems being added gradually. Foliage and flowers are added to the design either above or under-neath the tying point: materials to the left on top and materials to the right underneath. As the design progresses, all the stems will revolve, thereby creating the spiralling movement (the stems of the bouquet must spiral to achieve the lift and depth required in a bouquet to be carried over the arm).

Some of the lilac stems and the long arching branches of the exochorda are positioned to take full advantage of their natural angles. The freesia is concentrated in the part of the bouquet where the bride will be able to appreciate the full potency of the fragrance. To finish the design, the asparagus fern is carefully placed to tumble over several of the flowers, further enhancing the wispy effect of this delicate bouquet. All the stems can finally be tied firmly together and ribbon or raffia added.

Materials are placed at the outer edges and are built in towards the focal area.

PROFESSIONAL TIP
The shortened stems of the bouquet can be placed in water right up to the time the wedding flowers are to be delivered. Some of the lily stems can be gently smoothed between finger and thumb to help them curl.

Spring Bridesmaid

I t is the florist who adds the finishing touches to the wedding scene and particularly to the principal participants. This handtied posy links with the bride's springtime cascade of lilac and lilies while providing an individual and special design for the bridesmaid. Its domed shape is reminiscent of posies of the 19th-century German Biedermeier style, in which all the flowers are tightly packed together. Handtied designs have been carried at wedding ceremonies for centuries and it is perhaps this style of posy that most closely resembles those early bunched flowers.

CHOICE OF MATERIALS

The designs for the attendants must coordinate with the bride's flowers. The link could be the shape of the design, the flowers or colours used, or a combination of these elements. Here, both the colours and flowers – lilac and arums – link the posy with the spring wedding bridal bouquet on the preceding page, while the design is also an informal handtied design.

The blend of vibrant colour and contrasts of texture make this posy a striking design in its own right. The lime green *Euphorbia robbiae* is an excellent foil to the matt surface of the sharp yellow arum or calla lilies (*Zantedeschia aethiopica*). The lovely fragrance of the white lilac, *Syringa vulgaris* 'Vestale', is an added bonus to its texture. To contrast with the flowers in the posy, foliage from the lily of the valley (*Convallaria majalis*) and dark leather leaf (*Arachniodes adiantiformis*) have been selected.

ALTERNATIVE FLOWERS

The flowers for this spring posy are dainty and fragrant. In place of the arum lilies, either white or lemon tulips could be used. Narcissi and perhaps freesia would add fragrance, while drumstick primulas would be excellent instead of the lilac.

PREPARATION

For a tied posy, all the lower leaves must be removed from both the flowers and foliage. It is advisable to wear gloves when stripping the foliage from the euphorbia as the milky sap may irritate the skin. Take all the foliage from the lilac; it does not last well and competes for moisture with the many tiny lilac flowers.

CONSTRUCTION METHOD

To make this domed posy, the stems need to be spiralled in such a way that the flowers appear at the sides of the posy. Begin the design with a calla lily and some of the euphorbia foliage; more stems of both flowers and foliage are then added to the binding point. As the design develops, the whole posy can be turned in the hand to allow the cut materials to be added evenly. The lily of the valley foliage is interspersed at regular intervals among the flowers; its matt texture and 'flat' green are a good contrast to the colours of the arums and the surface texture of the lilac.

To finish the design, the leather leaf is added almost as a frill around the edge of the posy. The final touch is to bind all the stems together with the raffia, which may be left as a decorative feature.

At this halfway stage the flower materials are almost horizontal to the tying point.

PROFESSIONAL TIP

Euphorbia will benefit from being conditioned in fairly warm water to seal in the milky sap. If the sap is not prevented from leaking, it can pollute the water and this can shorten the vase life of sensitive flowers.

By combining the posy with a matching garland of flowers to be worn in the hair, you will be following in the footsteps of countless others who have made flower designs for brides and bridesmaids throughout the ages.

Summer Waterfall

A spray of foliage and tiny blue flowers tumbles lightly over the lilies, roses and agapanthus in this sumptuous waterfall bouquet. The pinks and blues, with a touch of rich red honeysuckle, combine to make an appealing colour harmony for a hot time of the year. The overall shape of this design is not dissimilar to the ever-popular shower bouquet. The difference is in the style and the way in which the flowers and foliage are used.

SELECTION OF MATERIALS

To give the impression of water, several light and dainty types of foliage and flower are used. The willow-leaved pear (*Pyrus salicifolia*), catches the light and has a silver sheen that is perfect for the theme of this bouquet. Harmonizing with the pear is *Perovskia atriplicifolia* 'Blue Haze', its name perfectly expressing its effect when used. A rose pink astilbe adds to the texture and its frothy appearance emphasizes the theme. Lesser periwinkle (*Vinca minor*), an excellent small-leaved trailing foliage for all wedding work, and bear grass (*Xerophyllum tenax*) complete the light and dainty foliage that is required to cascade over the larger flowers. The pale pink flowers are fragrant 'Le Rêve' lilies and small spray roses, 'Evelien'. Stems of deep blue *Agapanthus* 'Intermedia' are used boldly in this design, and the final touch is the deep red of the honeysuckle, *Lonicera periclymenum* 'Belgica'.

ALTERNATIVE FLOWERS

An excellent alternative foliage for the waterfall is *Asparagus setaceus*; its lace-like fronds would be fine enough not to hide the flowers used. *Asparagus meyeri* would be a bolder selection, and would give the desired tumbling and cascading effect. Pastel colours are visually light and dainty, giving a cool feeling to a summer design.

CONSTRUCTION METHOD

This design is made on a manufactured foam holder that consists of a small piece of foam in a plastic cage, with a handle for carrying the bouquet. The plastic foam is lightly soaked in tepid water to which cut flower food has been added; this will maximize the life of the flowers, which is severely limited by the very small reservoir of water available. Starting at the tail of this design, some of the lighter and daintier materials can be inserted, some of the larger single ivy leaves being added for visual weight at the centre. For extra security, the vulnerable and longer heavy materials can be mount-wired and the wires returned back into the holder around the bars of the cage. Make sure that the stem ends are cut at a sharp angle and inserted firmly into the foam. As the design develops, some of the light foliage is inserted so the trails tumble over the larger flowers. The design builds towards a focal area and it is at this stage that generous amounts of the dainty materials are added. Finish the bouquet by checking the overall shape and profile.

LEFT Build the bouquet by adding flowers and foliage from the bottom or tail upwards.

RIGHT All the cut materials should appear to cascade forwards, with no backward-facing materials.

Summer Scents For a Bridesmaid

Posies, pomanders and tied bunches are among the popular wedding designs carried by child bridesmaids. A basket of flowers, however, is often the perfect choice, as it is so easy to adapt to the theme of a wedding. A carefully-chosen selection of natural-looking flowers and foliage in a rustic basket will enhance a country-style wedding, for example, or you might fill a basket with a seasonal combination, such as tulips, muscari, ranunculus, *Narcissus* 'Cheerfulness' and mimosa for a wedding taking place in the spring.

CONTAINER

Baskets are now available in a range of shades, colours and sizes and may be made of rustic branches, smooth cane or slatted wood, as used in a traditional garden trug. For this summer wedding design, the choice was a slightly oval basket woven from dark willow. The basket is firmly made, with a solid high handle, and will hold the foam, flowers and foliage securely. A plastic lining is already attached to it; this is a bonus as it saves time which would otherwise be spent trying to make the basket waterproof.

CHOICE OF MATERIALS

Love-in-a-mist (*Nigella damascena*), trails of honey-suckle (*Lonicera periclymenum*), dainty astilbe, *Dianthus* 'Prudence' and lavender – all summer flowers – are used to create the outline shape. The rich plum-coloured foliage of *Cotinus coggyria* 'Royal Purple' fills the basket and provides visual depth. Small spray roses, 'Pink Delight', and scabious provide the central interest. These materials are dainty and in scale with the basket and the size of a young bridesmaid.

Select a range of flowers and foliage with dainty shapes and forms.

ALTERNATIVE MATERIALS

For a winter wedding with a colour theme of old gold and cream, a wicker basket could be lightly dusted with old gold spray paint and then filled with gold ranunculus, white roses, *Euphorbia fulgens* 'Yellow River', small pieces of blue pine, spruce, artificial berries and small gold lotus seed heads. A gold chiffon ribbon would add a seasonal touch.

CONSTRUCTION METHOD

Assemble the flowers, foliage and basket together with foam that has been pre-soaked in a solution of cut flower food. Insert the stems of honeysuckle, astilbe, lavender and nigella to form an outline. Add short stems of the cotinus foliage in the centre. Create a slightly domed shape by adding stems of fine materials, such as lavender, astilbe and honey-suckle, taking care to leave space for the bridesmaid to hold the basket handle. Add the roses and scabious and recess some cotinus foliage. Fill in with dianthus, astilbe and honeysuckle at various levels. Rotate the basket and check that there are flowers and foliage on all levels.

PROFESSIONAL TIP

Flowers and foliage are placed on all levels; this is particularly useful when it is carried by a young bridesmaid, for at whichever angle she holds the basket, the design should always photograph well. The colours must harmonize with those of the bridal bouquet.

Floral Passion

Flower garlands are one of the most universal ways of displaying flowers, being found in most cultures throughout the world. Sometimes they are used to adorn a person, for example the Polynesian *lei*, given to visitors as a welcome gift, or the garlands used for both bride and groom in a Hindu wedding ceremony. In many societies they are frequently used to decorate an architectural feature. A garland may be hung around a room at Christmas, or trailed up a staircase to set the scene for a wedding reception. The garland here is draped around a beautiful wooden beam that offers a rich texture in the open grain of the wood. In this instance, the flower-garlanded wood structure makes a dramatic free-standing design that is easily moved and could be used in a wide range of locations, such as at an hotel or in a marquee.

CHOICE OF MATERIALS

The garland is attached to a free-standing weathered piece of wood, which becomes an integral part of the design, contrasting beautifully with the soft textures of the flowers and foliage. The plant material is chosen to give a fresh summer-garden impression, the main flowers being the pink lily 'Le Rêve'. The mid-pink rose 'Pink Tango' is added low down, and the rich blue *Scabiosa caucasica* 'Stella' adds a vibrance to the colouring. The base foliage is soft *Ruscus*, while flowers and foliage trails of the climbing passion flower (*Passiflora caerulea*) complete the design.

ALTERNATIVE FLOWERS

Flowers with a roundish, solid form are needed. The lily 'Stargazer' could be used if a deeper pink flower is required, or alternatively an open-headed gerbera, such as 'Sabrina', with its striking combination of soft pink petals and black centre, could be substituted for the lilies. Lime-green *Alchemilla mollis* could take the place of the soft ruscus, while sweet peas, such as 'Royal Flush', would contribute the essence of a summer garden.

CONSTRUCTION METHOD

The base for the garland is a series of open plastic mesh tubes attached together to form a chain. Each tube is filled with wet plastic foam, which supports the whole range of fresh plant materials. The weathered wooden beam, about 1.5m (5ft) high, is cemented into a plastic pot and the base is later covered with moss and foliage. The garland is attached with a nail at the top of the wooden beam, spiralled downwards around the trunk, and secured with a wire at the base. This makes the design movable.

The ruscus, along with scabious and hydrangea, is used to create the frame and shape of the garland.

PROFESSIONAL TIP
The garland can be easily transported if laid in a flat flower box that is lined with polythene to keep in all the moisture. The garland can be made at a convenient location, where it can be kept fresh, and attached in position at the last minute.

Purple Haze

This deliciously colourful wedding bouquet, with flowers and foliage in plums and vivid pink, is a strikingly unusual combination for autumn, when the cool air at this time of year makes us want to wrap ourselves up against damp chill mists. The colour of the *Rosa rugosa* against the dark velvety purples is both distinctive and warmly comforting. The design is rich in detail, with a combination of dark purple plums, black shiny elderberries and two varieties of ornamental cabbage. These unsophisticated materials provide an effective contrast to the opulence of the roses and the pretty star-shaped flowers of the tricyrtis. The richly-tasselled trails of love-lies-bleeding add a distinctive texture and form to this bouquet.

CHOICE OF MATERIALS

The tremendous amount of detail in this wedding bouquet adds to the feeling of an almost baroque splendour. Among the typically autumnal flowers included are *Aster novi-belgii*, statice (*Limonium sinuatum*), *Buddleja davidii* 'Empire Blue' and *Hydrangea macrophyll*a. The strong pink foliage of *Cordyline fructicosa* 'Prins Albert', works well with the cabbage leaves, while the rhododendron rosettes offer a contrast in colour and shape. The berries with the misty blue bloom are *Berberis gagnepainii*. A very intriguing flower that is as yet only available in small quantities is the *Tricyrtis formosana*. Its common name – toad lily – just does not do justice to this pretty and long lasting flower. The focal point of the bouquet,

however, is the *Rosa rugosa* commonly called the Ramanas rose, which has a wonderful fragrance, shape and colour that make up for the simply horrible thorns. The rose buds, too, are quite elegant in their shape. Love-lies-bleeding (*Amaranthus caudatus*) adds a rich velvety texture to the design that complements the other flowers and foliage well.

ALTERNATIVE FLOWERS

In autumn there is a tremendous range of flowers and foliage in the perhaps more obvious colour choice of vibrant and fiery reds and oranges. A seasonal and popular combination might include straw-coloured cereals, such as wheat, barley and the dainty seed heads of oats, which would offer a contrast to red and orange berries, and spikey, flame-coloured dahlias.

PREPARATION

Give all the materials a long drink before beginning the design. Collect all the items required, such as the ribbon and the foamholder. A selection of stub wires and a glue gun will also be needed.

CONSTRUCTION METHOD

The foliage and some of the berries are placed to form a framework for other materials. A suitable gauge of mount wire, either 0.70mm (22g) or 0.90mm (20g), is required to secure the stems of the amaranthus trails to the plastic cage. The plums are secured by fixing two wires across the base of each. Wooden picks could be used as an alternative to the wire; whichever method you use, the bouquet will benefit from touches of glue from the glue gun for extra security.

As the design builds up towards the centre, a wire-edged ribbon is ruffled and ruched just off-centre to the holder and attached with a wire mount and a little glue. Some ribbon trails beside the amaranthus. Put a little cling film or cellophane beneath the ribbon as it is secured to prevent it soaking up water. Add flowers at different levels to achieve a full, rounded width. The roses almost complete the design, which only needs to be held and turned around for a final check to ensure there is a good textural contrast. The foam can then be sprayed with water from a mister bottle.

A flower box can be recycled to deliver the bouquet safely and attractively. Cover the box with paper, fill the inside with soft tissue paper, and rest the bouquet on top. Make a 'tent' of cellophane to cover the bouquet without touching the flowers. When the flowers are delivered, the bride and her family can see the bouquet, yet the flowers will be protected from the chill autumn air.

The first materials are inserted into the holder around the outside edge first, and then placements are made towards the centre.

PROFESSIONAL TIP

The flowers and foliage are inserted into a manufactured foam holder while the foam is dry. When the design is complete, the foam can be sprayed with water to give it a thorough soaking. One distinct advantage is that flowers, foliage and sundries can be glued in place for extra security.

An attractive ribbon is ruched and pinned to the foam holder. Plastic film or cellophane can be used to protect it from getting wet.

Winter Wedding

T he traditional season for weddings is lengthening and the wish to be different, coupled with the difficulty of securing the ideal venue, has encouraged many couples to opt for a winter wedding. Richly-textured fabrics in gold, oranges and greens are often chosen for bridesmaids, and many brides select gold brocade for their dresses.

CHOICE OF MATERIALS

This bouquet is given a rich winter feel by selecting flowers in burnt orange and gold from the warm side of the colour wheel. The feeling of moving from winter into spring and the promise of new things to come, so

appropriate for a wedding, has been achieved by using strong fresh green foliage. The choice of apricot parrot tulips for the main flower also helps. The texture of the bouquet is made more interesting by the inclusion of berries of *Mahonia* x 'Charity'. Trailing and twisting stems of Chinese gooseberry (*Actinidia chinensis*), an easy-to-grow wall climber, give the whole a wild and natural look.

ALTERNATIVE MATERIALS

A number of vine-type plants with a climbing or scrambling habit, such as honeysuckle, *Wisteria sinensis* and greater periwinkle (*Vinca major*), could provide the natural twisted stems that frame the bouquet. Roses, such as either the soft gold 'Safari' or the paler 'Osiana' would be effective as a focal flower.

CONSTRUCTION METHOD

The bouquet is made on a wet foam holder. This allows it to be made in advance yet remain fresh on the wedding morning. To achieve a loose, natural look, an outline of *Actinidia chinensis* is placed in the foam first. The tulips are then added to create the focal area, and the rich winter feel is provided by berries and foliage.

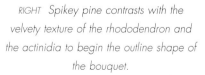

RIGHT Spikey pine contrasts with the velvety texture of the rhododendron and the actinidia to begin the outline shape of the bouquet.

LEFT Tulips, roses and foliage develop the design, with shorter stems of foliage covering the holder.

PROFESSIONAL TIP
The plant materials placed at the outer edge of the bouquet should be wired into the plastic cage of the foam holder for added security.

Ideas for hand tieds

Adaptable style

Many people believe that the handtied assembly is a relatively recent European invention. In fact, the origins of the small tied bunch can be traced back to medieval times, when it had specific use: the tussie mussie was a small bunch of fresh pungent herbs and sweetly scented foliage carried by royalty or gentry, who believed that the plague was carried in foul air. The designs that follow illustrate how far the humble posy has come since those early days, for the handtied is currently one of the most versatile, popular forms of arrangement.

INNOVATIVE TECHNIQUES

Design styles evolve all the time, and new and different techniques are currently being incorporated into the handtied assembly. This can be seen in the Valentine's gift, where the heart frame has been combined with handtieds of red roses. Stem and branch structures are seen in three of the following handtieds, each with cut materials integrated to create unusual and eye-catching designs.

The idea of tightly-packed roses with their heads all on the same level is one way of creating a design with flowers of a single type. The mermaid posy is an example of this, and here the stems have been over-wrapped with tulle and golden wire. Framing or caging adds another dimension. Bear grass, over-wrapped with gold wire, is used to enclose the posy of captured roses, drawing the eye back towards the flowers.

The nursing staff in hospitals, clinics and nursing homes find that a handtied design is a convenient gift for a patient, who need only place the ready-arranged bunch in a vase. The method of aqua-packing a handtied means that the stems are constantly in water

A metal frame gives a jaunty angle to this heart while supporting stems of cherry blossom and golden ivy.

while being delivered, helping to prolong the vase life of the flowers and foliage.

The circular handtied is now replacing the flat pack bouquet wrapped in cellophane as an ideal gift. Added impact and customer satisfaction is achieved by gift wrapping the handtied in layers of coloured tissue paper and cellophane.

THE VERSATILITY OF HANDTIEDS

The handtied assembly is a highly adaptable style of design, with many different uses, and you will find handtieds not only in the following chapter but throughout this book. It is currently the fashionable design for weddings, for example, enabling small bridesmaids to carry dainty natural posies while the bride carries an over-the-arm tied bouquet. A natural-looking tied assembly, known as a sheaf, is now often chosen by friends, neighbours or colleagues as an appropriate sympathy tribute, while the deceased's family may ask for a sheaf of just one type of flower, such as beautiful long-stemmed roses, or crisp white arum or 'Casa Blanca' lilies.

The tied assembly is, of course, an excellent contract design and can be made to any size to suit any location. Small handtied posies are more pleasing than a single stem of gypsophilia and a carnation spray in the specimen vase on the restaurant table. An exciting and flamboyant design of contorted branches, amaryllis or ginger, with complementary foliage would make an eye-catching design for a reception desk. The availability of exotic and home-produced artificial and dried materials provides another exciting range of forms, colours and textures.

The possible combinations of materials are endless, so each handtied can be designed to the client's individual requirements – small wonder that handtieds now play an important part in any florist's portfolio of designs.

PRACTICAL GUIDELINES

For success with handtieds, it helps to bear a few general rules in mind. As with all designs, use fresh, good quality, well-grown flowers and foliage, free of pests and disease damage. Ensure that all the materials are correctly conditioned, allowing flowers to absorb water for several hours before using them. Handtieds are normally placed straight into water by the recipient, so remove all foliage which will be below the water level, to prevent the growth of bacteria, and always add a packet of cut flower food to every fresh design.

A major ingredient of success with handtieds is to select the appropriate flowers and foliage for the style of design. The waterfall, for example, requires flowers with pliable stems and trailing stems of foliage. These two elements are essential to the construction of this type of handtied, as the stems are woven through the structure to create the cascading and tumbling effect.

All stems must be firmly secured at the tying point. Pot tape will give a secure finish, although sometimes a more stylish and attractive finish will be needed. Raffia or ribbon bows will add the final touch.

Customers should be advised to re-cut all stems diagonally, using a sharp knife rather than scissors, which would crush and damage the stem ends.

LEFT A waterfall of arums and asparagus ferns is tamed by the framework of bare branches.

BELOW Willow captures a host of lilies and orchids.

Glorious Bouquet

Glory lilies are aptly named, and when they are teamed with other spectacular flowers the result is a design that is justly called a glorious bouquet. Lilies, orchids and ranunculus have been used here in such a way that the beauty of the sinuous stems can be fully seen and appreciated. The lack of any foliage and the stark bare branches serve to highlight the beauty of each flower. This delightful handtied bouquet would make a splendid gift for someone very special.

CHOICE OF MATERIALS

The strangely-shaped glory lilies (*Gloriosa rothschildiana*), and the waxy but richly-coloured calla or arum lilies (*Zantedeschia aethiopica*), provided the initial inspiration for this design. They are obviously linked by their colour, but also by their strong and unusual shape. To contrast with these striking flowers, the delicate and ethereal beauty of the orchid, *Oncidium* 'Golden Showers', was selected. The rounded shape of *Ranunculus asiaticus*, with its many layers of delicate petals, has a stabilizing influence. The flowers all have flexible stems in common. The branches used to form the structure or framework are bamboo (*Arundinaria*), black willow (*Salix moupinensis*) and birch (*Betula pendula*).

ALTERNATIVE FLOWERS

The secret of this handtied bouquet is to choose flowers with pliable stems. Tulips would be an excellent choice, as would love-lies-bleeding, with its velvety tassels. *Euphorbia fulgens* and *Phalaenopsis* orchids have good curving stems that lend themselves beautifully to this bouquet.

PREPARATION

Make a circle or small wreath of bamboo leaves by binding them with reel wire. To keep the circular shape and to support the stems, attach small but stronger stems of bamboo to the circle with raffia. Birch and black willow branches are inserted to provide an upright framework for the flowers. The branches are woven in and out of the framework and

ABOVE A bamboo circle acts as a boundary for the upright framework of branches.

LEFT The flowers appear to weave themselves in and out of the willow and birch branches, their spiralling stems enhancing the aesthetic qualities of this design.

attached with wire to each other and to the bamboo structure. They will provide areas of space within the framework and 'stems' for the bouquet.

The glory lilies will need to be gently teased apart. The tiny tendrils at the ends of the leaves will twine around anything they touch. All the flowers must be conditioned in tepid water with flower food.

CONSTRUCTION METHOD

Place the stems of fresh materials into the construction from above. When the stems are anchored in the hand the flower heads can be gently twisted and pushed into position. Use the structure to support and hold the flowers. As more flowers are added, it becomes easier to anchor the flower heads. The stems must spiral in

this design, not only for practical reasons, but because this is an integral part of the overall aesthetics.

Birch can be added as the design develops. The ranunculus are used towards the centre of the design, with the lilies and the orchids stretching to the outer edges, almost as though they are trying to escape the framework. To finish the design, tie all the stems together at the binding point with raffia. Ribbons, if used, should be kept very simple.

PROFESSIONAL TIP

Make the structure in advance. It can be formed from any material that is flexible and strong. Frames of this type can be used several times, but care must be taken to tighten the wires, as the branches will shrink a little with age.

Making an Entrance

The reception desk in an office complex, hotel foyer or banking hall is a vital area, where it is essential to provide a welcoming image. Many reception areas can look monotonous and lifeless because of modern furnishings and bland decor, but a large imposing handtied in the latest style of container will enhance even the most ordinary of locations. Fresh flowers and foliage, however, are not always suitable, as the atmosphere may be too hot or light levels too low. The answer to these problems is a handtied of dried and artificial materials.

CHOICE OF MATERIALS

Gone are the gaudy colours and stiff unnatural-looking flowers and foliage of former years. Here, bundles of tall reeds and tightly twisted ting-ting cane give the handtied a strong upright movement and act as a backbone. Large 'Casa Blanca' lilies create the overall shape and provide central interest. To one side, branches of lemons form an attractive grouping; these are counterbalanced on the opposite side by a burst of love-in-a-mist (*Nigella damascena*). Stems of bouvardia, large leaves and moss contribute visual depth.

CONTAINER

There are several factors which should be considered when selecting a suitable container, as this is an integral part of the overall design. A large handtied needs a tall, heavy container which provides actual and visual balance for the design. Here a tall, weighty vase of a semi-transparent chunky green glass is used in order to allow the tied stems, which form part of the overall design, to be visible. Always be aware of future, as well as present, trends in container style if you wish to ensure that you are creating the most innovative designs.

ALTERNATIVE MATERIALS

Remember to select upright materials to establish the height, striking flower types for the centre, and smaller but interesting materials to fill in. Trailing and flowing stems of flowers, foliage and berries will add visual movement, and solid leaves give visual depth.

CONSTRUCTION

Collect together the materials, twine and container. Establish the height by binding together the bundle of reeds and the two bunches of ting-ting cane. Create the width and strengthen the height with the 'Casa Blanca' lilies, and add lemon branches on different levels. Place two large lilies in the centre. Now add the burst of nigella and place three individual lilies behind this to complete the triangular shape. Recess the stems of bouvardia under the central lily. Add two large leaves on different levels to provide visual weight, and fill in with reindeer or lichen moss. Tie all the stems firmly with twine, and - adding another feature – tie all stems together again near the base. Place the bunch in its container and adjust the materials, if need be, to ensure that there are flowers and foliage on all levels.

Establish the height, side width and depth with a range of materials, starting with the reed bundle and bunches of cane.

Captured Roses

A bright and cheerful handtied posy is given a touch of class and style with the addition of framing. Framing the flowers and enclosing the space around them, and indeed around the whole design, makes this handtied look really different. The unusual curving chive buds and loops of bear grass make this a distinctive design to give as a gift to someone special. The colour linking of the lemons and limes and the contrasts of lilacs and blues combine to create a very attractive and individual handtied posy.

CHOICE OF MATERIALS

In this design, the *Aster novi-belgii* 'Cha Cha' links together the lemons, lime greens and blue violet. Two types of foliage have been used: *Weigela hortensis* 'Looymansii Aurea', which has light golden foliage, and *Hebe odora*, an intriguing small-leafed spike form. Like the flowers, they were carefully chosen to offer a contrast in texture.

'Frisco' roses contrast strongly in shape with the *Solidago* 'Tara', yet they harmonize beautifully in colour. The green hellebores give a round shape to the posy and the lilac buds contribute further texture to the design. The addition of the bear grass (*Xerophyllum tenax*) and the chive (*Allium schoenoprasum*), contribute enormously to the overall effect.

ALTERNATIVE FLOWERS

In the spring, *Ranunculus asiaticus* could be used, the smaller buds curving around the edge. An all-year-round choice could be button chrysanthemums (*Dendranthema*).

PREPARATION

The flowers and foliage for this design need to be conditioned in tepid water with cut flower food. The lilac and weigela will benefit from the special food for woody-stemmed materials. Remove all the lower foliage from the stems; crushed foliage below the tying point will only pollute the water and shorten the vase life of the posy.

The bear grass is made ready by winding some gold-coloured reel wire around the strands and fastening the wire at each end by twisting the wire around itself and the grass.

CONSTRUCTION METHOD

Holding the materials between forefinger and thumb, begin the posy with a rose and some of the bushy weigela. Add further stems of flowers and foliage to the posy, rotating the stems in the hand and adjusting the fingers holding the posy for comfort. By doing this, you find that you can place the stems into the tying point at an angle. This creates a spiralling effect that allows each flower head to have its own space. Individual pieces of the bear grass can be added, with the top end of each piece anchored into the tying point over the heads of some of the other flowers.

The rounded and domed shape of the posy is achieved by adding more and more flowers. When the final flowers are in place the outer loops of bear grass can be introduced, as well as the lovely closed buds of the chives.

Strands of the prepared bear grass are anchored and then looped across the flower heads in the design.

PROFESSIONAL TIP

Framing is a design technique that can be used to enclose space or to isolate individual flowers or areas of an arrangement, making the enclosed part look more important. A light wire, 0.46mm (26g), is inserted into the stems of the outer chives to keep the curved shape.

Mermaid Posy

T his delightful design, standing on its 'tip toes', would make a wonderful presentation gift. Large coral-coloured roses are interspersed with wispy fronds of astilbe and creamy cockleshells that are caught up in strands of gold-coloured wire. A large anthurium leaf brings to mind the green depths of a sea wave with the foamy sprays of fern tumbling over it. Glamour is added to the design with frothy tulle, making it comfortable and easy to hold. The posy is light in weight – an important consideration for any bouquet that is to be carried. Its soft colouring will match or contrast with a wide range of fabrics and colours.

CHOICE OF MATERIALS

The delicate coral of 'Toscanini' roses inspired this posy with its theme of the sea. The solid outline of an anthurium leaf gives the design a visual stability and balances beautifully with the long stem length of the whole design. It acts as a foil to the mass of roses and the stems of *Asparagus seteceus* and *Astilbe*. Sprigs of foliage of *Gaultheria shallon* are used at the back of the large anthurium leaf to complete the design.

ALTERNATIVE DESIGNS

A ballerina bouquet, a princess posy, a Snow White bouquet, or flowers for Thumbelina – any of these fairy-tale themes, with a little thought, would make an inspirational starting point for a delightful themed bouquet. Outrageous bouquets, filled with vitality and dashing design elements, could be evolved from record, film or television themes.

PREPARATION

The cockle shells are prepared by wrapping them with gold reel wire to make a long string of shells. Leave a sufficient length of wire between individual shells to allow plenty of flexibilty when taking the wire into the tying point and bringing it back up again.

As with all tied designs, it is essential to remove the lower foliage from all the cut stems. This is for two important reasons: firstly, when the flowers are placed in water there should be no damaged foliage below the water line to pollute the water, shortening the vase life of the flowers; secondly, any unnecessary foliage would merely add to the bulk at the tying point, which makes large designs, in particular, tiring to hold. Any thorns on the roses will need to be removed, and care must be taken with the backward-facing thorns on the asparagus.

CONSTRUCTION METHOD

Begin the posy with two or three of the roses. These are followed with the astilbe and more roses. In contrast with other tied designs, the stems are parallel and do not spiral. Strands of the wire with the cockle shells can be added as the design develops, the wire ends being tucked into the tying point. Add the asparagus and gaultheria and then the anthurium leaf, the last foliage to be added. The 'V' shape of the leaf is locked around the stems of the roses so that they appear to be coming out of the middle of the leaf. The design is then tied with twine, raffia or, if preferred, pot tape. A length of tulle is wrapped around the stems, and gold-coloured wire is criss-crossed over it. Finally, a bow is added at the tying point.

PROFESSIONAL TIP

The length of the stems, which gives this design its very distinctive and elegant feel, also makes it easy to carry.

Mango Colours in a Lead Cone

A futuristic design looks very effective in locations where the decor is clear-cut and understated. The minimalist style is now found in hotels, commercial and public buildings and private homes. The concept and essential characteristics of this design emulate a waterfall in its natural surroundings. Here, the river bursts over a flat range of rocks and descends rapidly from a great height, creating a cascade of billowing, swirling water. These qualities are evoked in an arrangement or handtied by giving the design a flat or slightly domed top and interweaving and over-lapping flowers, foliage and appropriate sundries, integrating them to produce a strong, cascading effect.

CONTAINER

An inexpensive glass vase is 'cone wrapped' with a piece of lead 40cm (16in) square, which is easy to manipulate. Gently lap the lead over the rim of the vase and the container is ready. The cone could be inserted into a metal tripod stand and filled with a waterfall handtied. Alternatively, attach a bracket to the cone, fix it to the wall, and then insert dried or artificial materials. Lead cones also look effective in pairs, particularly on each side of a mirror.

CHOICE OF MATERIALS

The vibrant arum, *Zantedeschia aethiopica* 'Mango', is perfect for this design, as its soft stems are easy to manipulate into the required position and the whirling effect of the flowers evokes the swirling water. The cage of willow (*Salix*) provides the overall billowing feeling. *Asparagus densiflorus* 'Meyeri' and *A. setaceus*, plus *Typha* leaves and bear grass (*Xerophyllum tenax*) are used for the overlapping and interweaving. Red roses, *Leucadendron* and rolled *Galax urceolata* leaves are recessed to give visual depth.

PREPARATION

Make a foundation frame by binding and securing willow lengths into a ring approximately 10cm (4in) in diameter. Attach two cross pieces of willow to a central length of willow. Secure these cross pieces into the centre of ring; then tie six equally spaced 76cm (30in) lengths of willow to the ring, with 12.5cm (5in) of stem length below the ring. Gather together the main central willow and two opposite lengths, and secure them with pot tape. To remove bulk and weight, trim the remaining lengths back to the ring. Now secure willow lengths at random to the top section, forming an arch and three-dimensional shape.

CONSTRUCTION METHOD

Start by weaving several pieces of typha grass through the framework. Insert the arums into the frame at various levels, passing the stems through the willow ring into the 'handle' section. Use the framework to position the flowers and foliage at different levels, creating the cascading effect. Use the long-stemmed materials to overlap short materials. Interweave the soft-stemmed grasses; recess some materials on lower levels to give visual depth, using 'enclosed' space as a feature to ensure that the design remains light and airy. Where necessary, secure materials, such as the arums, to the framework. This will give greater security and enhance the flowing lines. Bind the stems together and gently insert the finished handtied into its container.

PROFESSIONAL TIP

For the cage framework, select foliage which is flexible and easy to manipulate, such as willow or dogwood (*Cornus*). Use flowers and foliage which are naturally curved, as their flowing movement is more easily integrated into the framework.

Place the framework into the lead container to ensure it fits. Now start weaving pieces of foliage through the frame-work. It can then be secured with a wire which is coated with paper ribbon, making it both functional and decorative.

Romantically Inclined

Nothing says romance more than hearts and flowers on Valentine's day. Nowadays, flowers can be selected to reflect the feelings of romantics who want to reveal their love in an individual way — a sophisticated bouquet of lilies with lush green foliage, for example, simple tulips or roses, exotic orchids with tropical foliage, or a natural mixture of dainty spring-like flowers. Carefully-chosen flowers and foliage can be constructed in various types of handtieds or free-style arrangements. However, for the customer who appreciates the unusual and wants to create the maximum impact on their loved one, this large flower-covered heart, with handtieds of luscious red roses, will fulfil all requirements and give a new and exciting twist to the Valentine's day theme.

CHOICE OF MATERIALS

Branches of the white cherry blossom, *Prunus* x *subhirtella* 'Taihaku', creates a full heart shape. Trails of variegated ivy, *Hedera helix* 'Tonny', intertwine with the blossom. Twenty-four richly romantic 'Red Velvet' roses are added — a delight to capture any heart.

CONSTRUCTION METHOD

A large distinctive heart frame is shaped from heavy-gauge garden wire. Firmly secure the wire ends together with 0.56mm (24g) reel wire, over-wrapped with pot tape. Cover the frame with natural curving branches of cherry blossom, bound on at intervals with wire. Next, twist long trails of ivy through the blossom. Make two handtied bouquets of roses. Fasten one at the front of the frame; place the other at the back on a lower level. Add extra trails of ivy; secure each handtied firmly with pot tape, and finish with a raffia bow.

PROFESSIONAL TIP

Heavy-gauge garden wire is easy to use, and provides a good, positive heart shape.

ABOVE Cover the whole wire frame with branches of cherry blossom, secured with 0.56mm (24g) wire.

LEFT Entwine long trails of ivy through the cherry blossom, and attach a handtied of roses to the front of the frame.

Sparkling Fresh Handtied

The advent of cellophane and other clear plastic wrappings has been a great help to anyone who enjoys arranging gift bouquets. The wrapping is available on rolls 25m, 50m and 100m (approximately 25yds, 50yds and 100yds) in length. A wide range of colours and patterns is available, but often the plain wrapping gives the best results, allowing beautiful flowers to speak for themselves. One of the most useful developments has been aqua-pack wrapping, in which the waterproof properties of the wrapping material are used to the full by encasing the cut stems of the bouquet in a bag. This is secured at the tying point of the bouquet and is filled with water; the flowers are protected by the wrapping material but the stems are in water, so the bouquet is absolutely fresh when delivered. This is useful in many situations, such as a hospital, where a vase of the correct size may not be available.

CHOICE OF MATERIALS

Bright yellow arums (*Zantedeschia aethiopica*), 'Lemon Dream' roses and 'Connecticut King' lilies form the main flowers for this handtied bouquet. Accents are added with the brownish-red flowers of kangaroo paw, *Anigozanthos* 'Rufus Red', the orchid 'James Storey' and *Leucadendron* 'Red Sunset'. Foliage, including *Fatsia* leaves, adds visual weight to the bottom of the design.

CONSTRUCTION METHOD

This design allows each flower or foliage stem to speak for itself. The flowers are grouped rather than distributed evenly, so that the visual impact of each flower is strengthened. There are five groupings, set at differing heights and with different numbers of flowers; this allows areas of the bouquet

to remain distinct while still giving the whole a visual balance. The strong stems of kangeroo paw form the centre, the flowers spiralling around at different heights, giving interest to the finished bouquet. The design is tied at the binding point, and the stems are cut flat across the bottom so it can stand on its own.

A square of cellophane, large enough to form a bag around the bottom of the bouquet, is tied at the binding point with a 15cm (6in) lip projecting above the tie. The bag can then be filled with water to the half-way level.

LEFT The spiralling stems allow a generous space around the groups of flowers. The design looks equally attractive from all sides.

RIGHT Materials with natural curves are used horizontally to create width.

ALTERNATIVE FLOWERS

Select flowers with strong stems, such as liatris, spray chrysanthemums or solidaster. Spring flowers might include pussy willow, irises and hyacinths, with leaves of *Arum italicum*. More unusual alternatives would include anthuriums, heliconias, and cymbidium orchids, perhaps with contorted willow to add height.

PROFESSIONAL TIP

Add foliage with strong branches and leaves to the base of the main spine to help to separate the other groups.

Rainbow-Wrapped Roses

Gift-wrapping materials have never been so varied or spectacular as they are today. The new wrapping paper provides a fresh and exciting way to add design flair and impact to a hostess bouquet, natural posy, or pot plant. Different papers contribute another dimension in colour, shape and texture, so be bold and adventurous in your selection. Experienced, innovative designers can blend a variety of wrapping mediums together, such as rainbow tissue papers and tasteful cellophanes, or use to great effect papers with a metallic finish. Add the finishing touch of raffia, hessian, paper ribbon bows or even cords trimmed with tassels.

CHOICE OF MATERIALS

The complementary colour harmony of yellow and violet – here, a dramatic dark purple tulip 'Black Knight' and the lovely fresh-looking rose 'Lemon Dream' – has been used to attract immediate attention. Rich purple *Trachelium caeruleum* makes a substantial filler and further contrast is provided by the blue-green eucalyptus spikes. Soft mauve paper wrapping adds a delicate finish and creates a special gift.

ALTERNATIVE WRAPPING

Add extra special gift-wrapping by using various colour combinations. These could be coordinated to reflect the time of year; add seasonal variety to your designs by welcoming spring with lemon-yellow and lime-green wrapping papers or for a summer handtied, try pale and deep blues, pinks and soft violets. For an autumnal theme use orange, cream, peach and brown wrapping papers. To evoke the magic of Christmas with a jewelled look, combine reds, blues, purples and emerald greens; alternatively, gold and copper metallic papers can add a festive touch to a bouquet.

PROFESSIONAL TIP

As the stems are encased in cellophane and the paper wrapping is protected, about 1cm (½in) of water can be carefully poured into the centre of the handtied (see page 92).

CONSTRUCTION METHOD

Make a full hostess bouquet with an interesting choice of flowers and foliage. Tie it firmly and trim the stems. Cut a square of cellophane to suit the overall size of the handtied. Place the handtied in the centre of the cellophane and gather it up, encasing the stems. Secure the gathering with pot tape or twine. Then fold a length of wrapping almost in half, ensuring that you have two layers. Pleat the paper slightly and carefully place it around the handtied; secure it with pot tape or twine. Cut another, slightly larger square of cellophane and place the handtied in the centre; gather it up, and secure the gathering. Flute and pleat the cellophane so that it neatly overlaps the paper wrapping.

Wild and Wonderful Tropicals

This handtied, consisting of plant materials that are architectural in form, is perfect for the futuristic image of floral design and floristry. It can be placed in a variety of locations, ranging from the avant-garde private home, to working environments such as ultra-modern offices, banks, shops and hotels, where the effect required is simple yet dynamic and even exotic. When considering flowers and foliage, keep in mind the aim of this design, which is to create maximum interest, using striking, distinctive forms as well as unusual and exotic materials.

CHOICE OF MATERIALS

The most eye-catching materials here are the cone-like form, which is a shampoo ginger, and a pink *Banana musa*. Both are unusual and will certainly stimulate conversation, making excellent focal area materials. Triumphant strelitzia creates height and width, and the silky, shimmering silver-grey foliage of *Leucadendron argenteum* adds a soft textural quality. Visual weight is provided by the bold elegant anthurium leaves. The stems of heliconia and bamboo have interesting markings and a piece of fresh birch bark adds a textural quality. Finally, rich purple *Trachelium caeruleum* are grouped at the base to give weight.

CONTAINER

To achieve unity and harmony, care must be taken when selecting the container, which should echo the modernist theme without dominating the overall result. Here, the tall, cylindrical container, which is made from slightly transparent blue glass, provides visual balance for the bold design. It is also heavy and can support framework and materials of substantial weight.

CONSTRUCTION METHOD

To make the framework, overlap lengths of heliconia and bamboo into a series of triangles, tying stems together where they overlap. Assemble the remaining plant materials and twine, and remove all lower leaves from the stems. When making the handtied, remember all materials are inserted through the framework. To gain height, place two strelitzia, one below the other. Add the stems of leucadendron to the side and back of the strelitzia. Create the width of the design by adding another two strelitzia, counter-balancing these on the opposite side with two anthurium leaves. Position one anthurium leaf just below the central strelitzia. Most of the stems will spiral, but the shampoo ginger and pink banana musa stems are placed parallel to one another in the centre of the design.

Finally, tightly pack the trachelium to the front, below the ginger and banana. Secure all the stems of the handtied with pot tape, and then cut the stem ends diagonally. Insert the handtied stems through the space at the centre of the framework and then carefully ease them into the container. The framework will rest on the rim of the container.

Create the framework by using a combination of stems of various types.

special
event
schemes

Finishing touches

The successful completion of floral designs for special events is one of the most exciting aspects of a florist's work. It is an exhilarating experience to design for locations that may be as diverse as a fashionable restaurant, an elaborate corporate marquee and an elegant private home, where imaginative floral beauty adds the finishing touches to a promotional event, lavish reception or special party.

CREATING AN IMPACT

Whether the event is a fun Christmas party or a formal banquet, the floral decorations should provide an attractive welcome. The designs must enhance the setting, creating a happy and relaxed atmosphere in which the host and guests can have a memorable time. At conferences and promotions the floral designs have a different role. Close discussion with clients will reveal their priorities and suggest how floral decorations can emphasize a product or the corporate image, or draw attention to a conference platform.

PLANNING THE EVENT

Considerable knowledge and experience are required to organize a special event floral scheme. You must interpret the client's requirements, and a portfolio can be invaluable in showing the range of styles and flowers available. Negotiation of a budget also takes much skill. Many clients request lavish and complicated designs, not realizing the cost. It takes time and skill to explain the true value of a design and to devise a scheme that will match the budget.

First, establish the theme of the event. For a birthday party, the theme might be a tropical

Select flower arrangements that are bold and clearly visible, and will create a maximum impact.

forest, for which you which would require exotic flowers and foliage, with props chosen to capture the essence of the jungle. The focus for a wedding anniversary would be a specific colour combination. Magnificent top table arrangements and large, lavish pedestal designs are required for formal occasions, and the style of arrangement may well set the overall theme. It is most important that designs appear to be part of a scheme and not a jumble of unrelated ideas. Careful planning, however, will ensure success.

POSITIONING FLORAL DECORATIONS

Avoid scattering a large number of insignificant arrangements around the venue. To create the maximum impact, it is always more effective to site one or two highly impressive designs in prominent positions. Table arrangements are often an important feature. However, the guests will want eye contact and conversation with each other, so keep the designs well below or above eye level. Other features which lend themselves to decoration are quiet corners, pillars or mantelpieces, but take care that the designs will not damage the furnishings or the fabric of the building, nor hinder the movement of people.

THE VENUE

You should visit the venue at least once to help make critical decisions. A marquee can be a particularly difficult venue, as it is often only erected one or two days before the event. A quickly-sketched floor plan, with comprehensive notes, is an excellent aid when planning a scheme and should help you to identify any special fixtures, such as a dance floor, fire exits or radiators. Ask if there are positions where floral designs may not be placed. This will be important in churches and synagogues. You may need to visit the venue several times to finalize all the details with the client.

The venue decor may also suggest the choice of designs, types of flowers and the overall colour scheme. Take note of the colour of the furnishings, the table setting and linen, china or marquee lining.

Position arrangements in good light. If any artificial lights will be used, check the effect, especially if the event is an evening function in a church or hall. Candles are always in fashion, but advise clients not to leave them unattended.

PRACTICAL CHECKLIST

Make sure that you have the basic information. This may include a contact name and telephone number for the venue; entry and exit times; details of any necessary coordination with other people or events; health and safety procedures; security passes and parking arrangements at the venue; water supply; electrical points, and working area.

You will find it easier to work in an allocated area, where buckets and boxes of materials can be stored, as some designs will be better made in situ. Also ensure that you take plenty of dust sheets, dust pans, watering cans, sprays and rubbish sacks. Along with the other equipment in your workbox, you may need a glue gun, hammer and nails, power drill and extension lead, and you may also require a ladder.

WORK PLAN

Designing an appropriate scheme of floral decoration can be time-consuming, and the client will require a quotation. However, once the scheme is accepted, the buying list is placed with the suppliers and a work rota is prepared. Foliage and flowers may start arriving up

to a week before the event to ensure they are in peak condition. A work plan, detailing who does what and when, should include the conditioning of flowers and foliage, preparation of containers, completion of designs, delivery, and staging of the designs in situ. The organizer must review the completed scheme with the clients to ensure that they are satisfied. If a high profile guest is attending, you may also need to be at the venue during security checks, just in case last minute adjustments are required.

Finally, attention to detail is the most important feature of all successful special events.

Free Expression

The inspiration for this design came from a visit to a local scrap metal yard, which led to the discovery of a diamond-patterned metal mesh, an ideal base from which to develop a free-standing floor design. A dramatic angular design evolved, using materials in strong vertical and horizontal lines. The texture of the base of rusty metal and the repetitive pattern of the mesh strongly contributed to the finished product. This type of work is suitable for shop displays or stage settings, but its success depends on a clean and simple backdrop.

CHOICE OF MATERIALS

Strelitzia reginae leaves, with their strong forms, were chosen as the main interest for this piece, their colour contrasting with that of the metal frame. Accents of colour were added with black-centred sunflowers (*Helianthus annuus*), strong pieces of the yellow ivy, *Hedera helix* 'Buttercup', and small crab apples, *Malus* 'Golden Hornet'. The large, spear-shaped leaves and stems add a strong directional element.

ALTERNATIVE MATERIALS

The strong leaves of New Zealand flax (*Phormium tenax*) would be a good substitute for the strelitzia leaves, while gerberas or rudbeckias could be the main flowers. Various seed heads or small fruits, such as kumquats, could be threaded to take the place of the crab apples.

CONSTRUCTION METHOD

The metal support was made by welding two metal rods to the mesh and then welding these to a heavy metal base plate. This design does not rely on one dominant centre, but uses strong vertical and horizontal lines, formed by the strelitzia leaves, to create a number of areas of interest or multiple centres. Because the leaves are firm and will not wilt, they can be wired to the metal frame. Plastic foam holders (Oasis iglus) were attached at the crossing points of the leaves; this allowed extensions to the lines to be created by inserting pieces of ivy into the foam. These areas were strengthened by the round shapes of the sunflowers. Interest was added by crab apples threaded on 1.25mm (18g) wires, 25cm (10in) long, which were hooked at the end and hung from the metal frame.

LEFT Large, firm strelitzia leaves are attached to the metal frame to form the outline structure.

BELOW Strong lines of the leaves are strengthened with the addition of the crab apples and cut strelitzia stems.

PROFESSIONAL TIP

Condition plant materials
well before starting this type
of design as the pieces of
water-retaining plastic foam
are small. Alternatively, use
test tubes to allow the plant
material to have access to
reserves of water.

Summer Dream

Parties are fun occasions, and these days it is increasingly popular to have a theme, such as the Thirties, the Big Top or Arabian Nights. This dictates the menu and style of food to be served, the surrounding decor and, on occasions, what the guests should wear. Colour combinations are often used, for example, In the Pink, Black and White, or Out of the Blue. Flowers and floral designs are an important part of the party scene, and nowadays flowers, foliage, fruits, vegetables and moss can be fashioned into almost any shape or style. Whatever the chosen theme, the imagination can run wild - a designer's dream! But flights of fancy must be tempered by practicality and budget. Here, the chosen theme is a Midsummer's Night, with the emphasis on an abundance of English summer flowers and foliage and the grey stone of English garden containers. The large main design was intended for a buffet table; the smaller candle arrangement, for the guest tables, can be viewed from all angles.

CHOICE OF MATERIALS

The secret of success is to select a combination of flowers, foliage and accessories which clearly illustrates the chosen theme. The iris variety used here is *Iris sibirica* and the lily is 'Orlando'.

CONTAINERS

The link between the containers is the grey stone, which makes a container heavy, but very stable. The large oval basket-patterned stone trough is capable of holding a great quantity of flowers and foliage. A plastic bowl is filled with bricks of foam and secured in the trough with pot tape. A stone bird bath, raised on a plinth, is used for the guest tables. As with the trough, a small plastic

Use the spiky forms of flowers and foliage to create a light and delicate outline.

bowl filled with foam is placed in the bath.

For large-scale special events, such as anniversary parties and weddings, a considerable number of table decorations will be required. Often, the florist will be asked to provide a range of containers for twenty or more table arrangements.

CONSTRUCTION METHOD

For the large main arrangement, prepare a stone trough, and collect together well-conditioned summer flowers and foliage. Use the spiky flowers, such as larkspur, foxgloves (*Digitalis purpurea*) and *Polygonum macrophyllum*, together with small irises, trails of honeysuckle and *Alchemilla mollis*, to create the height, width

and depth. Fill in the centre of the design by placing a selection of the materials at different heights on various levels. Add the lily stems, recessing one or two lily flowers, plus other flowers and foliage to give visual depth. Bring trails of honeysuckle over the rim of the container. Drape a length of tulle around the base of the container to give the feeling of early morning mist.

The complementary arrangement in the bird-bath is essentially a domed posy design with a candle acting as a central focus.

To continue with the party theme, a similar combination of flowers and foliage is used in the table arrangements.

PROFESSIONAL TIP

For the guest tables, set the scene by using decorative fabrics, such as tulles and chiffons, as overlays and sprinkling the fabrics with small gold or silver stars, or gold coins. A set of bird baths or similar garden ornaments can be used over and over again, and have the advantage that their weight prevents them from being knocked over.

Arrangement for a Business Function

Cool greens and velvety sophisticated reds are the colours chosen for this arrangement for a business function. For today's businesses, often located in high-rise offices or new industrial parks, traditional arrangements would look out of place. The clean-cut lines of the container and the strong bold shapes and colours of this design, which uses lots of space, are entirely suitable for an all-important visit or presentation. The design is a partner to the arrangement overleaf, following the same themes of colour and style.

CHOICE OF MATERIALS

Shiny *Anthurium andreanum* 'Tropical' offers a good textural contrast to the velvet surface of the small *Gerbera* 'Salsa'. 'Red Velvet' roses add to the air of sophistication and elegance, and are the sort of choice flowers often expected at an important function. Stems of snake grass (*Equisetum*) are grouped together and the groups are set off by the plain green lily grass (*Liriope muscari*) and the large shiny surface of the castor oil plant (*Fatsia japonica*). The dark burgundy foliage with its elegantly-shaped leaves is *Lysimachia*.

ALTERNATIVE FLOWERS

Clean lines and bold outlines are suitable for the modern office. Tropical flowers, in particular, are distinctive in form and shape and are often highly colourful. Examples include the bird of paradise flower (*Strelitzia reginae*), ginger (*Alpinia*), and heliconia.

PREPARATION

Soak blocks of plastic foam before cutting them to fit the container and strapping them firmly in place with pot tape.

Cut flowers must be well conditioned to withstand the hot, dry air of most offices.

CONSTRUCTION METHOD

This arrangement begins with the placement of foliage. Lily grass is placed in the central area, giving the impression that a whole plant has been used. Fatsia leaves are grouped to one side and their visual weight is balanced by the placement of the mini-gerberas. These use a tremendous amount of space, which is an essential element in this design. The roses are placed into the design slightly asymmetrically and in groups of two. Visually heavier, the red anthuriums are kept to the central and lower areas. Using basic design principles in different and exciting ways leads to the distinction and innovation that is important at this level of flower arrangement. To finish, a bundle of the equisetum is tied with gold cord and inserted into the design with a twist of wire.

PROFESSIONAL TIP

Soak the plastic foam in a flower food to enable the flowers to get maximum benefit from the top-up water. It will help, in the generally dry conditions of offices, to use an anti-transpirant spray that will cut the amount of moisture lost from the leaves and petals.

Corporate Launch

One of the most important points to remember about producing arrangements for business functions is to relate the flower designs to the atmosphere of the function. A dynamic, modern, forward-looking image is often what is required. The choice of container or the colour and type of flowers are among the main ways of achieving this by echoing the mood or evoking a strong corporate identity. A major point to remember is that the flowers are there to enhance the occasion, not take it over, and should be part of an overall image. Free-standing floor designs are often the most effective way of achieving this type of impact.

CHOICE OF MATERIALS

The construction of this design has a very strong outline, supporting the arrangement while giving a clean but simple image. The plain, flat, black panels look interesting on their own, but could easily be used either to display a company logo or to take some sort of wording to help emphasize a message about the function. Black was chosen as a strong background colour, which demanded a design using equally strong forms of flowers and leaves in a contrasting colour; bright red anthuriums and strap-like iris leaves give the right effect.

ALTERNATIVE MATERIALS

The flowers should have vibrant colours, strong straight stems and clear shapes, so as to accentuate the simple lines: strelitzias, gerberas, or helico-nias would all be effective; alternatively, if cost is limited try gladioli or liatris. Gladioli foliage, steel grass, palm, and pieces of golden or contorted willow could also be used.

The dramatic lines of the black stand are repeated with the bright red anthurium flowers and bold tropical foliage.

CONSTRUCTION METHOD

The stand was made from two pieces of 1cm (½in) plywood, each 30cm (12in) wide, one measuring 1m (39in) and the second 1.5m (59in). One end of each piece was cut at an angle of 45 degrees and one of the off-cuts was used as the front triangle. Another length of plywood was used to make two shelves which were fixed at different heights, separating the main panels and acting as supports for the flower containers. The whole construction was then painted with matt black paint. Flat black plastic trays, each filled with a block of plastic foam, secured the flowers on two shelves and flower stems were inserted at an angle of 45 degrees.

The iris leaves are bent sharply at right angles. Not only does this reflect the down-ward angle of the wood, but the space around each gerbera is enclosed. This is repeated with the steel grass, and echoed by the natural shape of the anthurium leaf.

PROFESSIONAL TIP

If a stage has to be decorated and time is limited, this can be a very quick way of creating something striking, as the arrangements can be made beforehand. Use flowers with a strong outline that can be seen from a distance; fussy plant materials would be lost and detract from the overall effect.

Children's Party

Let your imagination run wild! Young people have a greater acceptance of the informal, and will appreciate the wildest and most outrageous of styles. Choose materials not normally found in floral designs. Use metal, glass, wood, plastic – anything and everything that will work in the design – but be selective. If too many gimmicks are used the result will be messy, but use vivid colours, bold flowers and unusual combinations for maximum impact.

CHOICE OF MATERIALS

Nature provides the brilliantly-orange *Strelitzia reginae*, which creates the height here. *Delphinium* hybrids give central interest and intensify the blue of the container, which is echoed by glass pebbles and coloured water. Marigolds (*Calendula officinalis*) and oranges add splashes of vibrant colour. Bun moss and foliage cover the base mechanics and add a natural finish. Test tubes with holes at the top of each side are used.

CONTAINER

The container has a vivid Mediterranean blue colouring and high glaze, and is sufficiently deep to hold securely the base of the metal rod frame and several bricks of foam, while providing a surface area on which to distribute an attractive covering of fruits, moss and foliage.

CONSTRUCTION METHOD

Twist, bend and loop three pieces of pliable welding rod, 3mm (⅛in) in diameter, into different lengths. Make up some plaster filler. While this is thickening, secure the three rods together with 0.56mm (24g) reel wire, then cover the wire with pot tape. Finally, over-bind the rods with blue raffia to give a decorative finish.

Place the rods into the centre of a 15cm (6in) plastic plant pot and

Before adding the test tubes, ensure that the looped metal rods are firmly secured.

secure them with stones. Add a layer of filler, then more stones and a final layer of filler. Smooth the surface and leave the filler to dry, then place the plant pot in the blue container and surround it with bricks of wet foam. To hide the mechanics, pieces of bun moss are secured by hairpins of 0.90mm (20g) wire. These give a partial covering, leaving space for the fruits, flowers and leaves which are the final placements.

Attach test tubes at various levels by carefully threading the welding rod wire through the holes at the top. Now secure them by tightly wrapping thick twine around each tube and welding rod. Several blue glass pebbles are inserted into the tubes to enhance the colour. Add loops of bear grass (*Xerophyllum tenax*) to create extra visual movement. Firmly insert two strelitzia and the delphinium stems. Add marigolds, curls of orange peel, and more loops of bear grass to the tubes.

Complete the textured base by adding whole and sliced sections of oranges, groups of curled aspidistra and *Fatsia japonica* leaves, marigolds and rolled leaves of *Galax urceolata*. Add two single test tubes, again attached to the welding rods, one to the side and another suspended over the front of the container. Finally, add blue dye to four of the test tubes.

Flower Border

T he occasion is often the predominant influence when selecting a design style and choosing flowers. Several factors are important here. The occasion is a wedding and the building where the ceremony is taking place is a recently-built hotel. The window for which the flowers are intended is tall, plain and has a very narrow sill. A design with detailed interest is required to contrast with the plain background and surrounding decor. The narrow sill and modern architecture dictate a contemporary approach, yet the occasion demands a soft, romantic arrangement.

CHOICE OF MATERIALS

Modern arrangements often call for bold flowers with plenty of impact, but in this design those chosen are a little softer and more flowing, to reflect the occasion. Singapore orchids (*Dendrobium phaelanopsis*), will cascade over the front of the sill, along with a range of foliage including *Ruscus racemosus*, leather leaf (*Arachniodes adiantiformis*), and bear grass (*Xerophyllum tenax*). Other foliage includes cane palm (*Howeia fosteriana*), the round leaves of *Galax urceolata* and the spear-shaped foliage of the montbretia, *Crocosmia* 'Lucifer'. To ensure the detail in the design several flowers have been selected: *Dianthus* 'Delphi', an unnamed and beautifully fragrant oriental lily, the feathery spikes of the goats beard (*Aruncus dioicus*), 'Eskimo' roses, elegant stems of larkspur (*Delphinium ajacis*) and the unusual blossom-like flowers of *Tradescantia virginiana* 'Innocence'.

ALTERNATIVE FLOWERS

For a different occasion, the flowers could be bolder in colour and stronger in their form or shape. Rich oranges and purples, for example, in a design using *Liatris spicata* and *Limonium perezii* to provide the violets, with 'Compass'

lilies, *Euphorbia fulgens* and *Gerbera* 'Lambada' contributing the vivid oranges. Carnations and roses could be selected in either oranges or delicious red-violets. This colour change would result in a completely different mood.

PREPARATION

The container will not be visible, so a green plastic tray can be used. This is filled with blocks of plastic foam. All the flowers are conditioned before use. The cane palm requires plaiting (see page 154), but this can be done several days in advance.

CONSTRUCTION METHOD

Plenty of foliage is inserted into the foam in groups to give an edging to the base. Foliage at the back will help the physical balance. The taller flowers in the design are placed into the plastic foam in bold groups. These groups, along with the foliage at the base, help to establish an outline and set the scale of the arrangement. This makes it easier to follow with the other flower materials. The soft lines of the materials are reflected in the curves flowing over the sill at the front of the arrangement.

The groups of foliage that edge and outline the base are balanced with the upright placements of flowers and other foliage.

PROFESSIONAL TIP

Green and white is an easy harmony to work with, especially if a wide range of shapes is chosen. In this design, spikes contrast with bold round shapes. Texture is also important in an all-white design; here, the different textures work well together. The clean, crisp design conveys the right image for a wedding. Incidentally, many white flowers are more fragrant than their brighter counterparts.

Pure Fantasy

One of the most interesting and enjoyable jobs a florist can be asked to undertake is to create a theme for a party or celebration. The chair seen here was part of a theme for a fantasy party based on *Alice in Wonderland*. For themes like this to work successfully, the overall effect has to be eye-catching or surreal, often with an element of humour. The scale should be bold, but the effect must not be freaky or bizarre. A better effect can often be created by using a few large pieces rather than a host of smaller items which passers-by may not even notice. An element of surprise is achieved by distorting the shape of an old wooden chair.

CHOICE OF MATERIALS

The shape of the chair is altered by using stems of giant hogweed (*Heracleum mantegazzianum)* to form the base of the chair, giving texture and form to the overall design. For safety, these stems should be collected from the plant after they have dried naturally. A touch of humour is added to the design with the textured chair seat; this is created out of berries, seed heads, fruits and mosses, a splash of colour being added by open heads of begonia flowers. Sphagnum and bun moss fill the gaps between the hogweed stems and also give additional texture to the seat. Positioned by the side of the chair is a fountain column; this is also constructed of giant hogweed stems. At the top of the column, a base of moss and wire mesh supports *Crocosmia* 'Lucifer', with nasturtium (*Tropaeolum majus*) trails.

ALTERNATIVE FLOWERS

Willow or Japanese knot weed (*Reynutria japonica*) could be used for the chair and the fountain base, with black-eyed *Gerbera* 'Alexandra' and *Cytisus* x *kewensis* 'Killiney Red' as the main flowers.

CONSTRUCTION METHOD

Dried stems of hogweed were split and then glued to the chair, covering it and extending beyond the frame. Differing heights and lengths make it look quite surreal. A thin layer of plastic foam, cut from a design sheet, was covered with groups of plant materials to create a base with a rich colour and texture.

ABOVE A black bucket, inserted into the top of the hogweed stand, acts as a form of vase for the flowers and foliage, the stems being supported with wire mesh.

LEFT To hold flower stems, lengthening the life of the design, test tubes were placed inside the hollow lengths of hogweed attached to the chair.

Glowing Advent Crown

Christmas arrangements always look their best when made out of natural plant materials. A selection of the unusual and exotic flowers now available from many good florists became the starting point for this design. The well-loved Christmas colours – red, green and cream – used in a mixture of exotic and more traditional Christmas plant materials, give this advent ring a flavour that is out of the ordinary but still seasonal. With some adjustments to the selection of fruits and flowers, the design could be used for a harvest supper, Thanksgiving, or Halloween.

CHOICE OF MATERIALS

This arrangement started with the decision to use a pumpkin as a natural outer container. A toning but neutral colour allows the heliconias and the cream candles to become the highlights of the arrangement. The main plant materials are the heliconias; their spiky angular form dominates the design and all other plant materials are chosen to repeat and strengthen this spiky feel. Secondary materials include the noble or blue fir (*Abies nobilis*); this, together with some Spanish moss, is enclosed in swirls of the white-stemmed bramble (*Rubus cockburnianus*). Extra depth and tone is created by the addition of berries, cones and red peppers, the whole giving a crown-of-thorns effect. The arrangement is filled with grapes to double as a table centre fruit bowl.

ALTERNATIVE MATERIALS

The bramble could be replaced with willow or dogwood, and a range of fruit can be used in the centre; good alternatives include red apples, pomegranates, tangerines or kumquats. If you wish to eat the fruit, cover the centre of the foam with transparent food wrap.

CONSTRUCTION METHOD

The top third is removed from a dark green pumpkin and a 25cm (10in) plastic foam posy pad is sunk into the hollowed-out middle. Heliconias, which are normally around 85cm (34in) long, are pulled apart and the individual bracts inserted into the foam at varying angles to give a spiky, domed effect. Blue fir and Spanish moss act as filler materials, while cream candles, 10cm (4in) high, are supported on wire hair-pins, which are taped to the base and pushed into the foam.

Complete the design by cutting the bramble into sections and inserting both ends in the foam at various angles to create a swirling effect.

All that remains is to insert the lengths of bramble, while wearing gardening gloves.

PROFESSIONAL TIP

The white-stemmed bramble, with its fresh green leaves, is an eye-catching hardy plant, easy to grow in most soils. The thorns, however, are quite sharp, so do not grow it near paths or in areas used by children. Heliconias are tropical flowers and are best kept at a normal room temperature.

White and Lime Christmas

White, silver and lots of glass add sparkle to this arrangement. The design has a traditional Christmas air, but by using a range of greens from the palest lime to the darkest bottle green, and combining colour with the strong forms of the plant material itself, the overall effect is interesting and unusual.

CHOICE OF MATERIALS

The starting point for this design is the strong vertical line created by the stems of a bunch of amaryllis – the dark green stems, topped by the large white flower heads, are perfect in their own right. Further interest is added with a selection of seed heads, limes, pebbles and lichen-covered twigs. Some of the materials have been silvered to create highlights and link with the light reflected through the glass container.

ALTERNATIVE FLOWERS

Lilies, nerines, tulips or daffodils could be used, as they have limited side branches and good strong vertical central stems.

CONSTRUCTION METHOD

As amaryllis are used as a vertical bunch, the flowers create visual weight at the top of the arrangement, but the choice of container can help to lessen this effect. For this design, a glass container has been selected that has sufficient depth and stability to anchor the stems, and its shallow open bowl allows interesting materials to be added to the base of the arrangement. Set on a dark glass dish with a strong horizontal line, the arrangement is visually stable.

To bind the stems together, a plaited rope of vine stems and silver cord is attached at the top of the arrangement, spiralled tightly around the stems, and tied off at the bottom. The amaryllis are anchored by a pin holder, while the other materials are loosely laid in the bowl, which is filled with water.

PROFESSIONAL TIP

Allow the amaryllis to condition in deep water for at least two hours before arranging them. If the arrangement has to be made in advance, cover the cut limes with transparent food wrap and remove this just before they are required.

Twelve Days of Christmas

The natural look of the matt pottery container, its numbered rim suggesting the passing of time and the words of the traditional song, inspired this design. A low Christmas arrangement, suitable for a coffee table, and full of very chunky plant material, seemed an ideal choice to complement this unusual and slightly eccentric bowl.

CHOICE OF MATERIALS

The soft blue grey of the container is reflected in the choice of blue fir (*Abies nobilis*) – a truly Christmassy foliage. Among the other types of foliage in this arrangement are the upright ivy (*Hedera erecta*) and small twigs covered with lichen. Fir cones and a plaited raffia rope add further interest. The rich red of the aptly-named 'Cardinal' roses, grouped to the centre and right of the design, is complemented by the bold and solid-looking white flowers of *Hippeastrum* 'Ludwig Dazzler'. The overall effect is visually bold and richly evocative of Christmas.

ALTERNATIVE FLOWERS

Scots pine would be appropriate for Christmas foliage. Carnations, either the scarlet red of *Dianthus* 'Scania' or the deep burgundy of *D.* 'Joker' could be substituted for the roses, and as an alternative to the hippeastrum, you could use 'Casa Blanca' or 'White Mountain' lilies. You could even use white poinsettia stems taken from a plant. Points of interest could be created with groups of walnuts or holly berries.

CONSTRUCTION METHOD

The bowl was filled with plastic foam, with sufficient space left at the back of the design to allow water to be added. The materials were inserted into the foam in groups and lines in order to create interesting areas within the design to attract the eye. The cones and raffia rope were attached to 0.90mm (20g) wires and pushed into the foam.

PROFESSIONAL TIP

After you have finished with the arrangement, dry the *Abies noblis*, which will last for years, and can be used again as an alternative to fresh foliage the following year. Similarly, the plaited raffia and the lichen-covered twigs can be saved and re-used in later designs.

Extending
the boundaries

Natural innovation

In recent years, there has been a reaction against the pressures of modern living, coupled with exposure to the natural world through books and television programmes. Whereas people used to appreciate majestic scenery, large mammals and splendid gardens, we have now become increasingly aware of the beauties of the insect world, the wonderful colours and textures of lichen on stones and wood, and every detail of the natural environment.

Intricate detailing contrasts with the visual simplicity of this design of bear grass, cornus, muscari and arums.

detail is introduced by the grape hyacinths and lilies of the valley, and the bowl becomes an essential part of the design – in a sense, its environment.

Beautiful use of texture is seen in the Christmas design for the stable door, where the background provided by the old wooden door is integral to the design. The importance of the right setting for any piece is explored in the white rose flower arch, where the garden intensifies the effect of this design, in which the test tubes that hold the roses contrast with the natural surroundings. This romantic arch provides a wonderful illustration of the way in which mechanical supports can become an integral part of any design.

INNOVATIVE DESIGNS

This has had a considerable impact on art and design. Many among the new generation of sculptors, artists and craftsmen are influenced by a way of looking at stones, rocks, metals, bark, leaves, stems and flowers in which these are appreciated for their individual, natural beauty, and as parts of an intricate web of ecosystems and environments. These influences are filtering through to mainstream floristry and flower arranging, and many people are interested to discover how designs incorporating these new ideas are made and are excited by the effects that can be created.

This chapter introduces some new techniques and shows a range of designs that are simple in approach but effective. A key ingredient of success with such innovative designs is a clear awareness of the elements of form, line, space, texture and colour. The spiralling arrangement in a blue glass bowl, for example, with its strong overall form and shape, relies on the contrast between the simplicity of the arum lilies and the fine spiralling lines of the willow and bear grass; intricate

FORM AND LINE

Initially, we are often drawn to its colour as the most visually dominant factor in a design, but if we take time to stand back for a critical look, analysing the value of its various elements, we recognize that the form and shape of the plant material and container has greater effect. A simple and very effective excercise is to photograph some designs with a black and white film; when they are stripped of their colour, the value of form and shape are seen. Whether straight or curved, thick or thin, line adds movement to an arrangement. When selecting the plant material for a design, straight strong lines, such as those created by New Zealand flax (*Phormium tenax*), can dominate a design; this can be used to great effect to provide a strong vertical, horizontal or diagonal along which the eye will travel. If both ends of the line are returned into the design, the eye will travel along the line and be taken back to the arrangement, so a returning line holds the attention longer than an outward-leading one.

SPACE

When deciding how much space to give an individual flower or leaf, the desired overall effect of the design must be clear. If a closely-packed domed or textured finish is needed, the dominant outlines will be those of groups or sections rather than individual flowers; in fact the effect may depend on individual plant materials having limited space. On an everyday basis, the best example of this is a field hedge, in which separate plants merge in the overall effect of the hedge outline.

Less closely-packed designs allow the individual leaf or flower to contribute to the overall design, and the looser style brings depth and a more layered effect. Whether the design is loose or packed, an arrangement must be displayed with sufficient space around it to allow it to be fully appreciated.

TEXTURE

Plant textures contribute a great deal to a successful arrangement. As a good starting point, plant material can be divided into three textures – fine, medium and coarse – and this applies to any arrangement, no matter what its scale. A particular plant, however, may fit into several categories. For example, the leaves of *Griselinia littoralis* can appear to have a coarse texture when used in a small arrangement or a fine texture when seen in a large free-standing design. If the aim is to have a dominant texture within an arrangement, then the majority of plant materials should have this texture. Contrast can be achieved by varying the textures used.

COLOUR

This is the element of design with which people are most familiar. There are general rules that can be followed; these use recognized colour harmonies and contrasts that the eye finds easy to read, but a great deal of fun can be had from experimenting with colour. Moods can be created and emotions stimulated, and the resulting effects may be very satisfying, so push out beyond the accepted boundaries, and try out new ideas and ways of looking at flower arranging.

ABOVE Several design elements are combined in the experimental bouquet.

RIGHT Repetition is the key to this windswept design.

Walk on the Wild Side

D ue to its softness and malleability, lead can be one of the most interesting materials with which to create containers, supports and structures for use in flower arranging. The ability to create a unique container can inspire people to think about design ideas and opens up new possibilities. This design started with playing around – the word playing is used deliberately, because designing should be a process of enjoyable discovery – with some lead sheet about 40cm (16in) in width and 1m (1yd) long, and seeing the shapes that evolved.

CHOICE OF MATERIALS

A range of strap-like leaves was chosen to reflect the curving arch of the lead. They needed to be sufficiently pliable, when attached at one end and twisted over the structure, to take on a gradual curve. The most solid leaf was New Zealand flax (*Phormium tenax*), the variety chosen being one that has a linear varigation that accentuates the sense of movement. This pattern was strengthened with iris leaves and red hot poker (*Kniphofia*) flowers.

ALTERNATIVE FLOWERS

Leaves of liriope or aspidistra have a suitably strap-like form, while arum lilies or tulips would reflect the sense of movement essential to this design.

LEFT Once pieces of foam have been secured to the lead frame, outline grasses and leaves can be added. The heavier grapes may need to be secured with wire.

BELOW Stems of orchids and glory lilies develop the design.

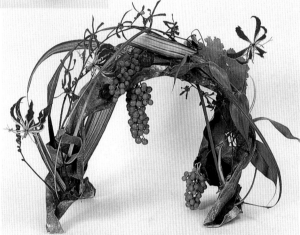

CONSTRUCTION METHOD

Ordinary roofing lead, which is readily available from many builders' merchants, is suitable. The first stage is to bend and twist the edges to improve the shape. Cuts are then made along the lead, and the edges are bent inwards to create an interesting pattern of solids and voids. A bridge or arch shape evolved here, and the four leg supports were formed to improve stability. Because of the way in which lead bends, wells and cradles can be created to take pieces of plastic foam or test tubes which will later be used to support plant materials. With this method, structure and container become one, and interesting designs evolve.

PROFESSIONAL TIP

Cover the base of the plastic foam with polythene to retain the moisture and extend the length of time the design will stay fresh. The plastic foam can be secured by pressing small pieces of lead against its surface.

Moss Sculpture

The ability to create moss shapes has traditionally been prized by floral designers, although the introduction of foam-based shapes led to a temporary decline in this skill. Recently, however, the interest in natural materials has inspired a revival of the art of moss sculpture. Based on the stone-carved bowls of fruit used as ornaments in many English gardens from the 1700s onwards, these sculptures – for that is what they are – will stand the worst of weathers outside, but are ideally placed as an amusing accent in a conservatory, summer house or loggia.

CHOICE OF MATERIALS

The base of each fruit is made from sphagnum moss, which is easily moulded into wire-bound shapes. These are then covered with a fine bright-green sheet moss. The fruits are grouped together or suspended from branches of contorted willow (*Salix matsudana* 'Tortuosa') and combined with camellia leaves, which will dry easily.

The choice of a stone container and stone-coloured plinth enhances the effect of a classic garden sculpture.

ALTERNATIVE MATERIALS

Small pieces of box or yew foliage will easily bind into shapes, as will grass, hay or straw. The ideal choice of base material to form the overall shape often depends on the size of the item to be made; any leaves should be quite small in order to create the fine details of the finished article, such as the characteristic shoulder of a pear. A more permanent structure can be made with a wire mesh base.

The fruits are constructed from sphagnum and sheet moss, plus reel and stub wires.

CONSTRUCTION METHOD

Being soft, the moss will take up any shape, while the binding wire helps to define and retain that shape. For the best results, choose simple geometric shapes, such as fruits, vegetables and simplified animal forms. Make a ball of moss and wrap it with 0.46mm or 0.56mm (26g or 24g) binding wire.

More moss can be bound in; the size of the shape will depend on the type of fruit you have chosen. If you start with small items, such as making grapes for a bunch, you will gain confidence and a feeling for the materials. Pull a 0.71mm (22g) hooked florists' stub wire through the fruits to allow the individual items to be secured in groups. Individual bunches can then be taped with florists' tape and attached to a branch.

PROFESSIONAL TIP

To retain the overall definition, do not over-crowd the bowl; to be effective, each item needs its own space. A final position against a plain backdrop will help clarity.

Blue Vortex

One of the innovations to come into floristry in recent years is the use of branches, twigs and strong stems to create a framework or structure as the basis for an arrangement. This opens up the possibility of creating unusually-shaped designs reflecting the strong shapes of some of today's containers. The framework also allows the floral designer to weave and twist soft-stemmed materials between the branches, which may have an attractive colouration and texture in their own right, and so create an unusual and interesting lattice-work effect.

CONTAINER

Choose a shallow dish about 5cm (2in) deep by a minimum of about 30cm (12in) across. The flowers and stems are woven in a band around the edge while still keeping the centre of the dish clear. The advantage of this is that the water in the container can then become an integral part of the overall design. Here, a glass bowl has been chosen so that the water will catch the light and reflect through the glass, enhancing its rich deep blue colour. This design is best viewed from above and should be placed at a low level – on a coffee table, for example.

CHOICE OF MATERIALS

As with most designs, one object or idea inspires the combination of materials. The rich blue of the glass container was the starting point, coupled with the strong fresh green of the *Cornus stolonifera* chosen for the framework. The bold curving shape and greenish white of the arums (*Zantedeschia aethiopica*) contrast with the container, while the flower stems strengthen and repeat the bright green of the cornus.

The finer and lighter blue flowers of the grape hyacinth (*Muscari*) reflect the colour of the container. These are woven with bear grass (*Xerophyllum tenax*) to strengthen the plant material.

ALTERNATIVE MATERIALS

For the framework, you could use willows in a range of colours, *Cornus alba,* vines, or a range of climbing plants. Choose flowers with fine, pliable stems, such as tulips, lily of the valley, small roses or gerberas.

CONSTRUCTION METHOD

For a circular design, the materials are kept to the rim of the container or bowl, with the centre kept free of all woven materials. The framework of branches can, if necessary, be wired together with florists' fine reel

ABOVE A side view of the design will allow guests at the table to appreciate the arum flowers and the beauty of their stems.

LEFT The design, seen before the placement of the last arum lily. The centre of the bowl will remain clearly visible, and is an integral part of the design.

wire. This is hidden by adding leaves and stems as the design develops, which may also help to create the open circular shape.

Use fine, pliable twigs or stems, with an open-branched habit and an attractive colour or texture that will contribute to the overall design. The framework should be a simple, basic skeleton, allowing other softer-stemmed flowers to be woven through, enhancing the intricate effect of the finished design.

Because the container is shallow, some of the branches are bent down into the water to form an anchor against which the flowers and leaves are lodged, keeping them in the water.

PROFESSIONAL TIP

Make sure the flower and plant materials chosen for this swirling type of design have soft and pliable stems so they will prove easy to weave.

Positive Charge

A table setting, either for lunch or dinner, can be enhanced by a multi-centred table arrangement. Beautiful clay pots, linked by contorted willow, evoke the feeling of an electric charge passing through the individual elements of this design. The result has a positive sense of movement and would be a talking point at any dinner party.

CHOICE OF MATERIALS

The rich terracotta of the containers was the trigger for this arrangement. Tints, tones and shades of orange predominate, accented by the complementary colour of lime green. The exotic flowers are a variety of heliconia with beautiful arching stems. The effect is of movement in one direction, as if all the materials are electrically charged, an impression strengthened by the contorted willow (*Salix matsudana* 'Tortuosa') and dried spathes of *Philodendron bipinnatifidum*. Orange 'Belinda' roses and flowers of the snowball tree (*Vibernum opulus* 'Sterile') add visual weight.

ALTERNATIVE MATERIALS

The orange freesia 'Escapade' or the cactus dahlia 'De Ruyter's Sensation' would look just as eye-catching as the heliconia. *Dianthus* 'Ministar' or mini-gerberas could replace the rose and the lime-green could be repeated by using *Alchemilla mollis, Amaranthus caudatus* or *Nicotiana* 'Limelight'. Stripped periwinkle (*Vinca major*) stems, or the flame-red flowers of *Euphorbia fulgens* could be woven through the design as an alternative to contorted willow. Later in the year experiment with heads of *Hydrangea hortensis* instead of the viburnum.

CONSTRUCTION METHOD

The clay pots were lined with polythene and filled with plastic foam so that stems could be easily inserted. The partially-dried outer guard spathes from the philodendron were taken and allowed to twist into interesting shapes as they dried completely.

The windswept framework of willow and philodendron spathes will enclose heliconia and other materials.

PROFESSIONAL TIP

Lime green can act as a highlight and lift many colour combinations. Store the dried spathes and use them in later designs. Make the design on a flat, thin piece of wood; you can then slide the finished piece gently off the wood and onto the table.

Anthurium Swirl

D elicious green anthuriums, shiny and dramatic, offer a complete contrast to the intricate weaving used in this design. The tapestry-like decoration around the jug, with its closely-woven details, inspired the arrangement within the jug. Foliage stems and seed heads are woven with branches, grasses and a sweet-smelling honeysuckle. The seed heads of radish add a froth of lightness to the whole arrangement.

CHOICE OF MATERIALS

Anthurium andreanum 'Midori' or painter's palette is an impressive contrast to the plain green lily grass (*Liriope muscari*), and the bear grass (*Xerophyllum tenax*). Repeating the weaving of these grasses is a cream and green grass, *Molina caerulea* 'Variegata'. Flowers of the honeysuckle (*Lonicera*) echo the seed heads of the radish, and both have gently curving stems. The bare branches of Japanese maple (*Acer palmatum*) are weathered, with moss and lichen shading the stems. A burgundy-coloured raffia has been used to link the arrangement with its container.

ALTERNATIVE FLOWERS

It is important to choose strong, bold and dramatic flowers that will contrast with the tapestry effect. Large oriental lilies, gerbera and cactus dahlias, with their spiky petals, will be effective against the woven tapestry of the grasses and branches. A very special choice would be stems of *Phalaenopsis* orchids.

PREPARATION

Cover the jug with dark green clematis netting and attach it securely with pot tape under- neath and inside the lip. Then the fun can begin: bear grass, lily grass, raffia, moss, a little conifer and the burgundy maple leaves are woven in and out of the netting. There is no need to attach or fix any of the materials as the netting holds everything in place securely. The final flourish is a little gold-coloured bullion wire taken around the jug.

The foundation for the arrangement is plastic foam enclosed in a manufactured plastic cage. This is attached to the jug with fix, a very sticky clay that can be purchased in strips or reels. The pot tape securing the netting will enable the fix to be removed without marking the jug. Once the dampened foam bump is attached securely, stems can be inserted.

CONSTRUCTION METHOD

The branches are placed in first. The struts of the plastic cage can be used to support them, and they then form an outer framework into which the other materials can be guided. The grasses are positioned and inserted next, followed by the seed heads, which are woven into the structure. The honeysuckle is tucked in, its foliage helping to hide the mechanics as its curving stems twist their way in and around the design.

The prepared jug is an enjoyable work of art in its own right.

Finally, the stiff straight stems of the anthuriums are inserted, the swirls of the other materials giving the impression that the anthuriums, too, are moving and swirling. Rhythm and visual movement are important elements in this design, and give it a vitality that is fascinating and almost mesmerizing.

The anthuriums and honey- suckle will benefit from regular misting with water to keep them in good condition, and the foam will also need to be thoroughly wetted each day.

The structure of branches supports the weaving of the remaining materials and echoes the textured tapestry of grasses around the jug.

PROFESSIONAL TIP

The jug tapestry dries beautifully and can be used time and time again. The grasses and branches will last for months and the flowers can be replaced two or three times before the plastic foam will need to be replaced.

Glistening Droplets

U nusual ways of arranging flowers lend themselves to special occasions, such as parties and weddings, because they make people take notice and a striking design is a talking point in itself. A floral arch is just such a feature. The free-standing arch here has been designed to be placed outside in a garden, and the site and setting inevitably relate closely to the style, selection of plant materials and construction of the arch. This would make an unusual entrance to greet guests at a summer garden wedding.

CHOICE OF MATERIALS

To make the most of the beautiful dappled light and blend it into the setting, lush green foliage forms a major element of this design. 'Jack Frost' roses, placed in test tubes of water, suspended with natural raffia, give highlights of white and a fresh summery feel. The test tubes containing the roses catch the light and add a sparkle to the overall effect.

ALTERNATIVE FLOWERS

Single stems of a small white lily, such as 'Sterling Star', would look stunning; earlier in the year, white tulips could be used, such as the lily-flowered 'White Triumphator' or the peony-flowered 'Mount Tacoma'.

CONSTRUCTION METHOD

The first stage is to design a free-standing metal frame of the correct size (a local welder was commissioned to produce the arch seen here). The dimensions will depend on the setting you wish to use. For a design of this nature to be practical, however, you will need to have a minimum clear head room, after the materials have been added, of 2m (6ft 6in) and preferably 2.25m (7ft 4in). The cross bar of the metal frame should be around 2.5-3m (8–10ft) above ground level. Erected in situ, the frame was then swathed in jasmine and ivy trails, all tied in to create a bower effect. Glass test tubes were then tied with natural raffia and secured to various points all around the frame, forming loose groups. The tubes were filled with water and a single

rose was placed in each. In the finished, integrated design, the structure of the archway, the test tubes and plant materials become a magical flowery entrance, setting the scene for a special occasion.

Experimental Bouquet

On the catwalks in Milan, Paris, New York and London, outrageous fashions are paraded before us by the ultra-chic fashion designers. Many of the new creations are totally impractical and very expensive. Yet within twelve months these incredible styles have been softened, a touch of practicality has been added, the modified ideas are on sale in the High Street, and everyone is buying them. This bouquet has been designed to create just such a reaction - one which will be very mixed. It contains several unusual design features, such as the woven 'fin' of bear grass. A group of four test tubes forms a main design feature, while equally important is the handle, which is suspended beneath the main group.

CHOICE OF MATERIALS

The fin is made with bear grass (*Xerophyllum tenax*), which is supple and easy to weave. The florets of the *Aranda* orchid 'Mohona Gold' that are attached to it make a rich contrast. Small flowers and leaves are used to fill the test tubes. The velvet quality of the 'Astra' roses is counter-balanced by the blue-green spiky form of *Eryngium* 'Orion'. *Celosia argentea* 'Toreador' adds visual depth. Groups of tiny poppies hide the bases of the test tubes and give central interest. Seed heads of grape hyacinth (*Muscari*) add further interest, as do *Galax urceolata* leaves, *Buddleia globosa* stems, and trails of honey-suckle (*Lonicera periclymenum*).

ALTERNATIVE MATERIALS

A single *Ornithogalum* floret could replace the orchid on the bear grass fin. Double lisianthus or double tulips would recreate the shape of the roses, and could be combined with *Trachelium caeruleum* 'Blue Wonder', tightly grouped to give a visual depth. Thin stems of love-lies-bleeding might be used to create the cascade effect represented by the fin.

PREPARING THE TEST TUBES

Fill the large test tubes with combinations of small flowers, stems of narrow foliage, such as soft ruscus, and small rolls of *Galax urceolata* leaves, over-wrapped with gold; 'plug' each test tube with a small piece of moss to stop the materials falling out.

CONSTRUCTION METHOD

Assemble the various plant materials, test tubes, bear grass, pre-soaked foam holder, and string-coated wire. First weave the bear-grass fin (see page 155). Pass the paper-coated wires through the holes at the rim of each tube. Wire two together; attach the third tube, and then fourth. The group can now be wired to the top of the foam holder. The fourth tube is also wired to the bottom of the holder. Add the galax leaves; wire the bear grass fin and insert it behind the group of tubes. Add the roses, eryngium, muscari seed heads, celosia, and clear-cut groups of tiny poppy heads. Buddleia and honeysuckle add visual depth. Single florets of the 'Mohona Gold' orchid are glued to the grass fin.

Using paper-coated wire, firmly attach the filled test tubes to the foam holder.

PROFESSIONAL TIP
New challenges! A designer florist will always break rules and cross boundaries in search of new and futuristic styles. This is the really exciting part of a florist's work.

Festive Stable Door

A doorway that is attractively decorated at festive times of the year looks inviting and welcomes guests or customers to a shop, hotel or home; it shows people care. The design should reflect the style of the door or window and complement the overall architecture. The traditional wreath enhances many doorways with its strong symmetrical balance, but with a little thought and creativity, more unusual designs can easily be created. Made of oak with iron studs, this old stable door has an earthy, timeless strength that can take a dramatic treatment.

CHOICE OF MATERIALS

The selection of plant materials and style of decoration reflects the natural beauty of the door. The timeless feel of the heavily-textured wood and raw metal studs could be complemented by a modern approach to the decoration as long as the plant and other materials look earthy, solid and natural. This design concentrates on fruit, berries and seed heads. A range of copper piping and wires with a diamond-shaped grid of rusted iron links the floral design with the studs on the door. All of this is supported by a limited quantity of fresh and dried leaves and stems.

ALTERNATIVE MATERIALS

Stems of reynutria could be used horizontally as an alternative base, with a range of fruits chosen to offer a variety of shapes, colours and textures. Oranges, nuts and apples could form the base, while a few black figs would add interest and a touch of the exotic. To complete the design, the steel grass could be replaced with fine stems of purple willow (*Salix daphnoides*).

CONSTRUCTION METHOD

The copper tubing is shaped and fixed to a metal-meshed grid which will later be used to attach the decoration to the door. Dried stems and hairy heads of lobster claws (*Heliconia*) are threaded through the copper tubing to create a horizontal line. The heads were then attached and hung downwards. Extra copper tubing is wrapped around pomegranates to create a hanging cradle shape and rhododendron leaves are

rolled and bound with copper wire, reminiscent of Christmas tree decorations. Star fruit and oranges are added, as well as groups of steel grass tipped with either crab apples or holly leaves. Spanish moss (*Tillandsia usneoides*) and clematis seed heads are added as a filler.

PROFESSIONAL TIP

When attaching a less weighty door decoration, push two drawing pins into the top edge of the door. Wire, ribbon or string can take the weight and the pins can be pushed in flush with the door edge so that they do not get caught when the door is shut.

Cut Flower Care

Many customers judge the quality of the flowers and foliage that they receive according to how long they last in an arrangement or vase. Over many years, science has helped to develop methods and products that assist the grower and florist in maximizing the vase life of flowers and foliage. The latest discovery is the identification of the ethylene hormone gene which accelerates the ageing and ripening process.

BUYING CUT MATERIALS

The purchase of cut materials for a business is normally the responsibility of either a senior member of staff or the manager or owner. This person will know which wholesaler to use, which types of cut materials to buy and in what quantities, how much to spend and, most important, they will recognize the quality of the cut materials. Knowing whether a cut flower is, or is going to be, of good quality comes with long experience of handling and using cut materials, but there are plenty of pointers to help buyers, and close and thorough observation and knowledge of the goods, suppliers and products that maximize flower and foliage life will ensure that customers get good value.

PREPARATION

Before cut materials arrive in the shop, some advance preparations can be undertaken that will speed up the conditioning process.
● Have all conditioning equipment ready: scissors, knife, secateurs, cut flower food, clean buckets, mister, cloths, dustpan, brushes and rubbish bags. You will also, of course, need water.
● Have a clear area ready where boxes and bunches of cut materials can be easily stacked, where you can work safely, and where rubbish can be easily disposed.
● Prepare clean stock buckets of varying sizes with tepid water and the correct amount of cut flower food.

INSPECTION

This sounds like a long process, but in fact it takes seconds if it is done as the materials arrive or as they are conditioned. When flowers and foliage arrive in the shop, check that the materials tally with the invoice or the delivery note. As you tick off the boxes and neatly stack them, make a visual inspection. Remember that damaged boxes can mean damaged flowers.
● Look for corners that have been squashed; if you find any, check to see whether or not the flowers have been crushed.
● Loose bars or batons (put in the boxes to hold cut materials firmly) may have allowed flowers to move inside a box.
● Wet or damp boxes means that cut materials inside may be susceptible to moulds.
● Visually inspect wrappings and packaging for the same reasons.
Unpack the cut materials as quickly as possible, looking for healthy cut materials in good condition and flowers at the correct stage of development. Certain flowers won't open properly if harvested too early.

Flowers harvested too late will mature or 'blow' quickly and have a shortened vase life.

Any problems or discrepancies should be reported to the buyer, who can then decide whether to contact the wholesaler.

PRIORITIES

Each time you have cut materials to condition you will have priorities, so the type of flower conditioned first one day may be lower on the list the next day. In general, however, the order would be as follows:
● wilted or flaccid flowers
● short-lived materials, such as sweet peas or violets
● delicate materials that may get crushed if left
● expensive materials (don't take any chances!)
● cut materials that are required urgently for customers
● soft-stemmed materials before woody-stemmed ones
After these, cut flowers and foliages that have been dry packed should be conditioned. Last of all, condition flowers that have been aqua packed.

METHOD OF CONDITIONING

This is used on almost all cut flowers. There are some special conditioning methods for specific flowers and types of foliage, and wilted materials need extra encouragement to take up water and nutrients. Use a sharp knife to cut stem ends whenever possible. Scissors can be used, but they damage the stem ends by 'crushing'. Damaged stems encourage bacterial growth; using a hammer for any stem end is definitely not recommended. Use a professional bucket cleaner for vases, buckets and equipment; this will help to prevent stems being blocked with dirt and bacteria.
● Remove foliage that will be below the waterline so the leaves will not decay in the water.
● Re-cut the stem ends with a diagonal or slant cut using a clean, sharp knife. (A diagonal cut exposes a greater stem surface to the water, thus improving water intake. It also prevents the stem from standing flat on the bottom of the container, which would impede the water supply).
● Remove or groom any injured outermost petals and any broken branches.
● Place the stems in a clean bucket, holding clean water, with the appropriate amount of cut flower food.

SPECIAL CONDITIONING METHODS

Some cut flowers and foliage need encouragement to take up water and nutrients, and florists need to be able to identify various stem types in order to decide which method will be best. There are five basic stem types: woody or hard stems, semi-woody or firm stems, soft stems, hollow stems and latex-producing stems.

WARM WATER TREATMENT Use this method with soft stems, firm stems, dry-packed materials, tropical cut flowers and flowers in tight bud. The warm or tepid water contains fewer oxygen bubbles and is absorbed by the stems faster, so that wilted and dry materials recover more quickly. Add some cut flower food to the warm water.

HOT WATER TREATMENT Use this method with woody, latex-producing and hollow stems, and to revive wilted materials. Stems are placed in a shallow depth of hot water, 80-90°C (140–155°F), for two minutes, after which the container is topped up with cooler water to which cut flower food has been added.

BURNING, SEARING OR SINGEING This method is slightly more time consuming and is therefore not used a great deal in florists' shops, but it can be useful with latex-producing stems, such as those of the euphorbia and poppy families. After cutting the stem ends with a knife, pass each stem end briefly through a flame and then place into water with cut flower food. The searing of the stem end forms a charcoal layer that prevents further latex seeping out and polluting the water, yet is sufficiently porous to allow water through.

SUBMERGING Use this method with wilted cut flowers, tropical cut flowers and materials that require high humidity levels, such as violets and maidenhair ferns. Re-cut the stem ends and submerge the materials in tepid water for between a half and two hours, depending on the type of cut material. The tepid water should contain the correct amount of cut flower food. Do not submerge hairy foliage or grey foliage, which will loose its colour until dry.

STORAGE

Once flowers have been conditioned, they will need some time to have a drink before being used in designs or sold in the shop. Aqua-packed materials will generally require a shorter amount of time and indeed could be put on sale immediately. Dry-packed materials require longer – say, from four to six hours. This will depend on the types of flowers and foliage and the extent of their need to replenish their water supply.

Once conditioned, most cut flowers should be stored in a cool room, cellar or a florists' cold room (fridge) at 4-8°C (40–46°F). Many spring flowers will withstand a lower temperature – 2°C (35°F) – but carnations prefer

a warmer minimum temperature, around 8°C (46°F). Generally, tropical cut flowers do not like the cold and prefer an even room temperature at about 16°C (60°F).

What does a cool temperature do for flowers and foliage? Several of the natural functions – respiration, transpiration and the production of ethylene gas – are slowed down. A cool temperature also slows down the growth of bacteria and moulds (one reason we keep food in a fridge), but prolonged storage of flowers at low temperatures increases their sensitivity to ethylene.

There are flowers that cannot be stored at too low a temperature. Nerines and roses will show signs of 'blue stain' and will not develop beyond the bud stage. Orchids, too, prefer warmer storage conditions, and remember that flowers displayed in the window can suffer chilling injuries in the winter months.

Too warm a storage temperature results in flowers maturing quickly and a shortened vase life. Low humidity in the surrounding air increases the water loss from the stomata. If combined with a high temperature, this will make it difficult for the flower to take in enough water at the stem to compensate for the loss through the stomata, so avoid leaving cut flowers in hot dry air.

ETHYLENE GAS

Ethylene gas is an odourless gas that is a natural plant hormone. It is also known as the ageing hormone. Plants, flowers, fruits and vegetables produce ethylene, which they require if they are to mature and ripen. Too much of the gas, however, will rapidly age a flower. Some sensitive flowers, such as carnations and many other summer flowers, can wither and die overnight; others can drop petals, florets or develop yellowing

foliage. As flowers mature, their sensitivity to ethylene increases. Florists can limit the effects of ethylene by the following methods:

● Avoid physical injury to flowers.

● Avoid storing flowers with fruits and vegetables, as these produce high levels of ethylene.

● Avoid storing bud flowers alongside fully mature (ethylene rich) flowers.

● Ensure good ventilation and air circulation in the cold room or storage area.

● Use proprietary cut flower food, which contains an ethylene inhibitor.

BACTERIA

Several flowers are particularly sensitive to vascular blockage. This applies to flowers in which the stem water is transported through tubes that are grouped together in bundles. These tubes have partitions (a bit like our veins), and if the tubes get blocked, the result is wilting or 'bent neck'.

The growth of micro-organisms, bacteria, is one of the main reasons for vascular blockage, and in favourable circumstances these organisms can multiply very rapidly. As well as blocking the tubes, they can break down plant tissue, which results in slimy stems and smelly water.

FLOWER FOOD

Cut flower food is available in several different forms including powder, liquid and labels to which sugar is added in the vase water. For the professional florist, the dosing units that provide the correct amount of food, already mixed, are good for conditioning flowers on a daily basis.

As flowers and foliage are cut, the process of photosynthesis is interrupted. Flowers have very small food reserves and these need to be replenished regularly if the flowers are to open and blooms are to develop to their full potential. Many cut flowers are given a pre-treatment after harvesting by the grower. The florist can continue this care by using cut flower foods and encouraging customers to continue this chain of care. Commercial brands of cut flower food are by no means all the same, and specially-adapted formulas are available for florists to ensure that flowers do not reach their full potential before reaching the customer.

Cut flower food contains sugars to nourish the blooms, anti-bacterial agents to prevent blockages, acidifier to lower the pH in the water and, in some formulas, ethylene inhibitors. Some foods have been developed for particular flowers, such as bouvardia and gerbera. There is a special formula for bulb flowers that enables daffodils to be mixed with tulips. Another product aids the flow of water through woody stems, such as lilac and mimosa, and can even be used with Christmas trees. It is easy to see why today's cut flower foods are better balanced and more effective than some of the old-fashioned remedies, such as lemonade and copper coins.

AFTERCARE ADVICE

To continue the care you have given the flowers in your shop, it is important to advise customers on the correct care methods. Care advice can be given to customers verbally when they buy, and a care card and goodwill sachet of cut flower food will back up that advice. If designs are being delivered, it is essential to give a care card and cut flower food.

FLOWER CARE CHART

NAMES	STAGE TO BUY	VASE LIFE	CONDITIONING METHODS	REMARKS
Acacia dealbata Mimosa	half florets open	5-7 days	•leave polythene bag on while conditioning •cut flower food •woody stems	•mist regularly •spicy fragrance •can be dried
Acanthus mollis Bear's Breeches	most bracts developed	2-3 weeks	•remove all leaves •cut flower food	•prickly •no scent •can be dried
Agapanthus spp African Lily, Lily of the Nile	quarter of flowers open	1-2 weeks	•place in tepid water immediately •short cool storage •cut flower food	•some cultivars have a tendency to drop flower heads if allowed to dry out •no scent
Alchemilla mollis Lady's Mantle	tight clusters of florets	up to 10 days	•cut flower food	•no scent •can be dried
Alpinia spp Ginger	most bracts fully formed	2-3 weeks	•tepid water •high humidity •cut flower food	•slightly scented •do not store below 13°C (58°F) •mist with water regularly
Amaranthus caudatus Love-lies-bleeding	trails fully developed with good colour	7-10 days	•remove most foliage •cut flower food	•no scent •can be dried
Anethum graveolans Dill	fully developed	5-8 days	•cut flower food	•aromatic •not suitable for culinary purposes
Anigozanthos flavidus Kangaroo Paw	most flowers open	1-2 weeks	•tepid water •cut flower food	•stems can dry out easily •store at room temperature
Anthurium hybrids Painter's Pallette	spike /spadix almost fully developed	8-15 days	•warm water 20-25°C (72-82°F) •no cut flower food •high humidity •can be submerged for 1-2 hours	•reds have shortest vase life •do not store below 15°C (62°F) •keep temperature even
Antirrhinum spp Snapdragon	third of flowers developed	8-10 days	•cut flower food •remove spent florets	•ethylene sensitive •spikes bend upwards when used horizontally
Arachnis flosaeris Spider Orchid	two-thirds of flowers developed	1 week	•cut flower food •high humidity	•ethylene sensitive •mist with water regularly
Aquilegia spp Columbine Granny's Bonnet	half buds showing good colour	5-7 days	•cut flower food •remove spent petals	•ethylene sensitve •seed heads are attractive and can be dried
Aster spp Michealmas Daisy September Flower	half of florets on stem open	up to 10 days	•cut flower food	•remove most of the foliage
Banksia spp	fully formed	3-4 weeks	•woody stems •cut flower food	•do not store below 13°C (58°F) •easily dried
Bupleurum griffithii	third of flowers open in bunch	1-2 weeks	•soft stems •no special care	•can be dried
Calendula officinalis Marigold	half of flowers open in bunch	5-10 days	•soft stem •no special care	•can be dried
Carthamus tinctorius Safflower	most of flower open	1-2 weeks	•foliage is not long lasting •cut flower food	•can easily be dried

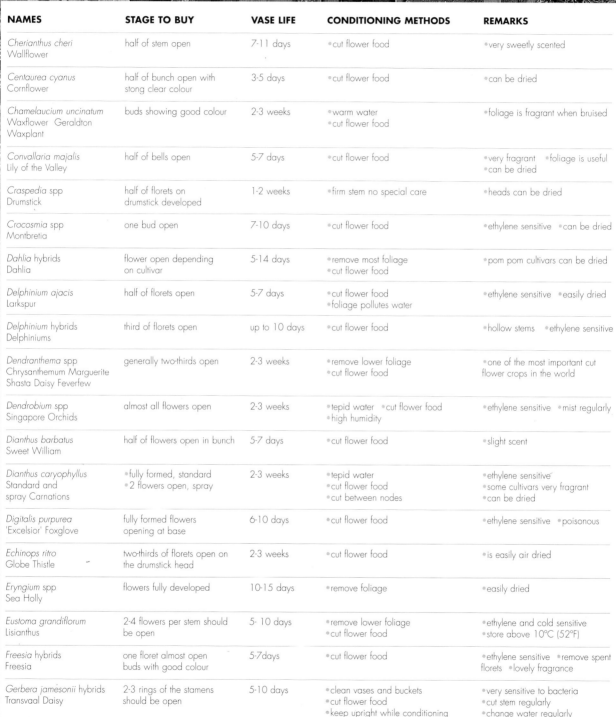

NAMES	STAGE TO BUY	VASE LIFE	CONDITIONING METHODS	REMARKS
Cherianthus cheri Wallflower	half of stem open	7-11 days	•cut flower food	•very sweetly scented
Centaurea cyanus Cornflower	half of bunch open with stong clear colour	3-5 days	•cut flower food	•can be dried
Chamelaucium uncinatum Waxflower Geraldton Waxplant	buds showing good colour	2-3 weeks	•warm water •cut flower food	•foliage is fragrant when bruised
Convallaria majalis Lily of the Valley	half of bells open	5-7 days	•cut flower food	•very fragrant •foliage is useful •can be dried
Craspedia spp Drumstick	half of florets on drumstick developed	1-2 weeks	•firm stem no special care	•heads can be dried
Crocosmia spp Montbretia	one bud open	7-10 days	•cut flower food	•ethylene sensitive •can be dried
Dahlia hybrids Dahlia	flower open depending on cultivar	5-14 days	•remove most foliage •cut flower food	•pom pom cultivars can be dried
Delphinium ajacis Larkspur	half of florets open	5-7 days	•cut flower food •foliage pollutes water	•ethylene sensitive •easily dried
Delphinium hybrids Delphiniums	third of florets open	up to 10 days	•cut flower food	•hollow stems •ethylene sensitive
Dendranthema spp Chrysanthemum Marguerite Shasta Daisy Feverfew	generally two-thirds open	2-3 weeks	•remove lower foliage •cut flower food	•one of the most important cut flower crops in the world
Dendrobium spp Singapore Orchids	almost all flowers open	2-3 weeks	•tepid water •cut flower food •high humidity	•ethylene sensitive •mist regularly
Dianthus barbatus Sweet William	half of flowers open in bunch	5-7 days	•cut flower food	•slight scent
Dianthus caryophyllus Standard and spray Carnations	•fully formed, standard • 2 flowers open, spray	2-3 weeks	•tepid water •cut flower food •cut between nodes	•ethylene sensitive •some cultivars very fragrant •can be dried
Digitalis purpurea 'Excelsior' Foxglove	fully formed flowers opening at base	6-10 days	•cut flower food	•ethylene sensitive •poisonous
Echinops ritro Globe Thistle	two-thirds of florets open on the drumstick head	2-3 weeks	•cut flower food	•is easily air dried
Eryngium spp Sea Holly	flowers fully developed	10-15 days	•remove foliage	•easily dried
Eustoma grandiflorum Lisianthus	2-4 flowers per stem should be open	5- 10 days	•remove lower foliage •cut flower food	•ethylene and cold sensitive •store above 10°C (52°F)
Freesia hybrids Freesia	one floret almost open buds with good colour	5-7days	•cut flower food	•ethylene sensitive •remove spent florets •lovely fragrance
Gerbera jamesonii hybrids Transvaal Daisy	2-3 rings of the stamens should be open	5-10 days	•clean vases and buckets •cut flower food •keep upright while conditioning	•very sensitive to bacteria •cut stem regularly •change water regularly

NAMES	STAGE TO BUY	VASE LIFE	CONDITIONING METHODS	REMARKS
Gloriosa superba 'Rothschildiana' Glory Lily	almost fully developed	12-14 days	•tepid water with cut flower food •high humidity •can be submerged	•easily damaged as tendrils on the end of leaves continue to cling •mist regularly
Heliconia spp Lobster Claw Parrot Flower	when bracts are fully coloured	1-2 weeks	•cut flower food •high humidity	•physical damage will shorten vase life •mist regularly
Hippeastrum hybrids	buds showing good colour	1-2 weeks	•hollow stems •cut flower food •do not store below 10°C (52°F)	•stem ends curl •use an elastic band to prevent stem shortening
Hypericum spp St John's Wort	most berries showing red/orange colour	2-3 weeks	•cut flower food	•berries last longer than foliage
Kniphofia uvaria hybrids Red Hot Poker	half of lower florets open	1-2 weeks	•cut flower food •store upright	•flower spikes bend upwards when used horizontally
Lathyrus odoratus Sweet Pea	flowers showing colour	5-7 days in cool conditions	cut flower food	•ethylene sensitive •delicate fragrance
Leucodendron spp Silvertree, Safari Sunset	when mature	2-4 weeks	•warm water •cut flower food	•some are easily air dried
Leucospermum cordifolium Pin Cushion Protea	when mature	10-15 days	•warm water, 15-20°C (62-72°F) •cut flower food	•can be dried
Liatris spicata Liatris, Gay feather	top florets open on spike	7-10 days	•cut flower food •foliage pollutes water	•ethylene sensitive •flowers from the top of the spike downwards
Lilium hybrids Lily	1-2 buds well coloured	1-2 weeks	•remove white portion of stem •cut flower food	•ethylene sensitive •many have wonderful scent • remove pollen anthers to prevent staining
Lupinus hybrids Lupins	half of florets on flower spike open	5-9 days	•hollow stem •sensitive to drying out •cut flower food	•tip bends upwards when used horizontally
Matthiola incana Stock Gilly flower	half of florets open on stem	5-7 days	•cut flower food •woody stems •foliage pollutes water	•ethylene sensitive •very fragrant
Moluccella laevis Bells of Ireland	papery green cups almost fully developed	2-3 weeks	•cut flower food	•can be air dried or glycerinèd
Muscari spp Grape Hyacinth	half of lower florets open	up to 7 days	•cut flower food •keep cool	•faint musk scent
Myosotis alpestris Forget-me-nots	half of the flowers should be open	7 days	•remove lower foliage •cut flower food	•keep cool
Narcissus hybrids Daffodils Jonquils	when the tight buds have just started to bend at the neck ('gooseneck' stage)	up to 7 days less when forced early in the season	•condition for 24 hours before mixing with other flowers unless special daffodil food is used	•ethylene sensitive •mucus causes harm to tulips, roses & freesia •do not recut stems •several cultivars are fragrant
Oncidium 'Golden Shower'	most flowers open	1-2 weeks	•cut flower food •high humidity •keep out of draughts	•ethylene sensitive •mist with water regularly
Ornithogalum spp Star of Bethlehem Chincherinchee	when lower buds are fully coloured	up to 3 weeks	•cut flower food	•ethylene sensitive •change water regularly

NAMES	STAGE TO BUY	VASE LIFE	CONDITIONING METHODS	REMARKS
Phlox spp Phlox	half of lower florets open	7-10 days	•cut flower food •top up buckets regularly	•ethylene sensitive •slightly scented
Physalis alkekengi Chinese Lantern	orange papery 'lanterns' fully developed	up to 2 weeks longer when dried	•remove foliage •cut flower food	•very popular as a dried flower
Prunus spp Flowering Almond, Cherry	buds showing colour	5-9 days	•cut flower food •woody stems	•can be forced
Ranunculus asiaticus Turban or Persian Buttercup	flower buds just beginning to open	5-10 days	•remove lower foliage •cut flower food •keep cool	•keep upright to prevent bending stems
Rosa hybrids Rose	in bud about to open	1-2weeks depending on cultivar	•remove lower foliage •remove lower thorns if being used for hand-held designs •cut flower food	•very sensitve to bacteria in the water •use clean equipment •change water regularly •some cultivars are fragrant •can be dried
Rudbeckia spp Coneflower	centres not fully developed	up to 7 days, centre of flower longer	•remove foliage •cut flower food	•sensitve to drying out •remove spent petals for an unusual flower head
Scabiosa caucasica Scabious	centres not developed	5-10 days	•remove lower foliage •cut flower food	•side buds often develop
Sedum spectabile Ice Plant	when florets are almost mature	up to 10 days	•remove lower foliage •cut flower food	•can be dried
Solidago and *Solidaster* hybrids Golden Rod	half flowers showing good colour	up to 7 days	•cut flower food •tepid water •remove most foliage	•can be dried
Strelitzia reginae Bird of Paradise	first flower open	2-3 weeks	•warm water •cut flower food •high humidity	•do not store below 13°C (58°F) •foliage is often sold separately
Syringa vulgaris Lilac	buds showing good colour	up to 2 weeks	•remove any foliage •cut flower food •top up buckets regularly	•keep cool •scented, especially purple and lilac
Trachelium spp Throatwort	almost fully open	7-10 days	•remove lower foliage •cut flower food	•sensitive to drying out
Tricyrtis spp Toad Lily	2-4 florets open buds showing good colour	5-10 days	•cut flower food	•no scent
Tulipa hybrids Tulip	buds should show some colour	5-10 days	•keep in wrapping to condition •cut flower food	•remove wrap after conditioning •top up buckets regularly
Veronica spp Speedwell	half of florets open on spike	5-7 days	•cut flower food •remove foliage	•sensitive to drying out •no scent
Viburnum opulus Guelder rose Snowball tree	florets should be a bright green	7-10 days	•remove foliage •woody stems	•sensitive to drying out
Zantedeschia hybrids Calla, Arum Lily	just as spathe is turning downwards and opening	up to 2 weeks	•cut flower food •keep cool but not cold	•an elastic band on the stem end will prevent shortening •light scent
Zinnia elegans Zinnia	fully developed flowers	5-7 days	•cut flower food •hollow stems	•can be dried •no scent

Techniques

FRAMES

With environmental issues making people more aware of the natural world, and with a major trend in floristry increasingly leading designers to a natural look, an addition to a florist's skills has been the relatively new design concept of encasing flowers within cages or open webs of stems and fine branches. Soft and supple-stemmed flowers and leaves can then be woven and threaded through this tracery, to create an open-textured effect that gives the design a great deal of depth and interest. This technique has been used here to create a beautiful arrangement and unusual formal presentation bouquet.

The frame of branches, grasses and golden wire forms the shape and adds structure to this design of tulips, freesias and roses.

CHOICE OF MATERIALS

The bouquet uses a bridy holder – a piece of wet foam encased in a plastic frame with a handle – as the base for the design, with pieces of fine rattan cane twisted and looped to create the cage. This is attached by wire to the plastic frame of the bridy holder. In this instance, the frame was sprayed gold, but often a natural look is best. Select fine open-leaved plant materials; solid forms block out areas, limiting your ability to create depth within the design. The 'Ilona' roses and the tassle-like *Lycestera formosa* add interest. The design is finished off with trails of natural-coloured raffia. Red tulips, such as 'Cassini', or a coloured ranunculus would also look effective, while the cage could easily be constructed from a number of shrubby willows, such as *Salix daphnoides* for a dark purple cage or *Salix chermesina* for a bright golden-orange one.

CONSTRUCTION METHOD

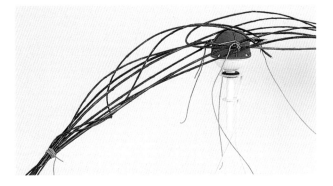

1 Select the cane and twist and loop it into a pleasing open design. One end can be attached to the cage at the beginning, which makes the twisting easier. If the cane is attached firmly in two or three places, the rest can be woven in and out to strengthen the structure. Do not make the caging too complicated as it is only a base through which the rest of the flowers and leaves are to be woven. It is the addition of the roses and foliage that will create interest.

2 Gauge the length of the roses by holding them up to the cage, and cut them accordingly, so that 2.5-5cm (1-2in) of stem can be pushed into the foam holder. Thread the roses through the cage with their stem ends first; this will avoid damage to the petals and will assist in the final positioning of the flower heads in relation to the cage. Fine asparagus foliage is added to create depth, and the design is finished with bunches of raffia inserted on wires into the foam.

OVER-BINDING

A new idea that is influencing the way in which we look at flowers and plant materials is the technique of over-binding. Any type of plant material can be used as the basis for this technique; it is, however, easiest to start with plant materials with a strong linear form, and these often produce the most successful results.

CHOICE OF MATERIALS

The plants used to illustrate this technique include bear grass (*Xerophyllum tenax*), broom (*Cytisus*), and rosemary (*Rosmarinus officinalis*). The over-binding is a soft 0.46mm (26g) reel wire in a shade of red. Fine stems of willow (*Salix*) varieties, birch (*Betula pendula*), dogwood (*Cornus*), greater periwinkle (*Vinca major*), and vineous stems, such as *Wisteria sinensis*, can all be used successfully.

Framing and over-binding are two skills worth acquiring to expand the repertoire of a floral designer.

CONSTRUCTION METHOD

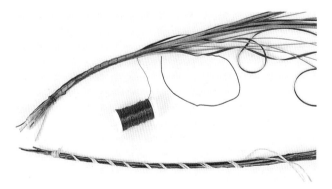

1 The technique is to bind or wrap a small group of leaves or stems, generally thin and narrow in shape, with another type of material. Wire, such as the red-coloured wire illustrated here, is often used.

2 To enable the bound rope to be twisted and manipulated into unusual shapes and loops, either use wire for the binding or place a wire inside the bunch before you start binding.

PLAITING PALMS

Plaited cane palm makes a distinctive addition to any design and prompts questions from the curious.

The plaited fronds of the cane palm (*Chrysalidocarpus lutescens*) are distinctive and look particularly effective in stylish modern arrangements, wedding bouquets and handtied designs. There are certain other palms that can be plaited: you might try the queen palm (*Arecastrum romanzoffianum*), or kentia palms (*Howea belmoreana* and *Howea forsteriana*), but the cane palm creates the best effect. The plaited fronds give a design a certain mystery as customers ask themselves and their friends whether or not it is real and what sort of plant it can have come from. Be warned, however, that once this skill is mastered, it can become addictive!

CONSTRUCTION METHOD

1 Place the reverse side of a palm leaf in front of you - the leaf should naturally curve towards you. As you hold the tips of the fronds, place the stem end on your tummy; this will support the leaf and give some tension. Begin by plaiting the top three fronds - the left one over the middle frond and the right over the new middle frond.

2 Now take the next left frond over the middle, and then another left frond is taken from the main stem over the middle. They must be pulled tightly, especially for a tight curl; the tighter the fronds are pulled, the more circular the final shape will be. Repeat the process with the right-hand fronds and continue plaiting all the way to the bottom of the stem.

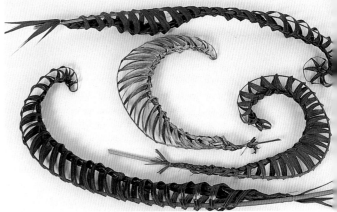

3 At the bottom of the stem, any loose fronds can be attached to the stem by tightly binding with reel wire, raffia, or twine.

PROFESSIONAL TIP

Cane palm dries well if hung upside down in a warm well-ventilated room. Check the binding point after a few days, as the fronds shrink as they dry. The drying time will vary with the room temperature, but should take about 10-14 days.

WEAVING GRASS

The beautiful effects that result from weaving bear grass (*Xerophyllum tenax*) are unique each time a piece is completed. Although it can be time-consuming, the distinctive results make this a worthwhile technique for very special arrangements or wedding bouquets, such as the one featured on pages 140-141. Other strap-shaped foliage can be tried; faster and bolder designs can be achieved, for example, using the rush-like leaves of typha, or the lily grass (*Lirope muscari*), although take care not to crack or break the strands of these fleshier grasses. The finished woven design can be dried for use with dried and artificial materials.

CONSTRUCTION METHOD

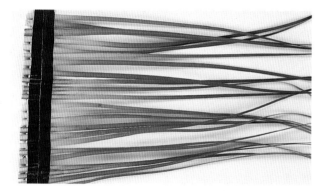

1 Several strands of bear grass, almost equal in length, are placed stem end down, side by side, on the sticky side of some pot tape. When the required total width of bear grass has been reached, a further strip of pot tape is placed over the tops of the stems.

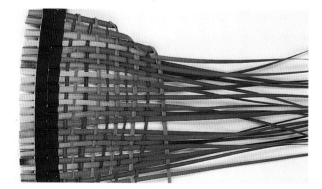

2 Begin by taking the outer strand from one side and weaving it across, taking it alternately above and below the other strands of grass. When you reach the opposite side, bend and turn the strand so it can be woven back to the first side. (Make sure the strands are pushed tightly against each other to achieve a close, strong and firm weave.) This is repeated until the weaving strand starts to get too fine. The end of the bear grass can be tucked into earlier weaving at either side of the design.

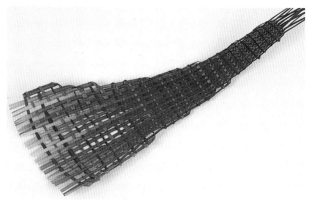

3 A new strand can be started either from the left or the right, and the process described in step one repeated. If strands are taken from just one side, the shape of the finished design will curve.

4 As the design gets narrower at the tip, the final strands of bear grass can be bound together with coloured reel wire or raffia and then neatly trimmed. At the stem end, the pot tape can be removed and the stem ends trimmed with scissors. The finished design can be rolled and 'stitched' together with an extra strand of bear grass so that the silvered reverse of the bear grass can be seen.

COVERED CONTAINERS

Ordinary, boring, plastic or chipped containers are easily re-vitalized. A total 'New Look' can be achieved by the addition of single leaves or lengths of cut stems to the outer surface of a container.

A simple earthenware jug assumes a new disguise, concealed with grasses, leaves, raffia and seed heads.

SIMPLE COVERINGS

Evergreen leaves, with their long-lasting qualities, are generally ideal for this purpose, but spectacular effects can also be achieved with the red and gold leaves of autumn. Suitable single leaves with which to create this instant transformation include laurel,camellia, ivy and galax leaves. Cut lengths of wheat, bamboo and willow can also be secured with this method.

1 A simple method of transforming a cheap plastic bowl is to cover the outside of the container with double-sided carpet tape.

2 Now firmly press single leaves onto the tape, making sure that you overlap the leaves slightly, hiding the container completely.

3 To combine added security with a natural-looking finish, tie plain or coloured raffia, coarse string or cord of the type used for curtain tie backs or cushion edging around the bowl.

TAPESTRY EFFECT

1 A soft green plastic netting tube (clematis netting) is secured with pot tape that is hidden inside the top lip of the container and tucked neatly beneath the base. Gather together a range of materials, which can include items such as berries, common ivy leaves, dried and fresh bear grass, seed heads, raffia and cord.

2 Carefully slide the ivy leaves through the mesh and place them flat against the container. The mesh will expand and contract quite easily to allow this. Now add clusters of berries and seed heads, entwining their stems through the mesh so that they are held securely. Weave in lengths of bear grass, raffia and cord. Continue to attach materials until an attractive finish has been achieved. With the exception of the berries, most of these materials will dry successfully. For a permanent finish, use dried and artificial items, which can then be sealed with clear varnish.

ALTERNATIVE MATERIALS

A wide range of weaving materials can be considered, including coloured wires, wool, thin strips of fabric, string, and plain or guilded cords. Dried or artificial leaves, berries or seed heads will add visual weight. Beads, pearls, shells and glass pebbles create interest and can be used to add sparkle and reflected light.

PAINT EFFECTS

The diversity of decorative paint techniques, such as dragging, sponging, splattering and rag rolling, has given the world of interior design a new style concept. Surprisingly, once these techniques are mastered they are often simple to use.

CONTAINERS

Paint techniques can be used to revitalize smudged, old and out-of-date containers, or to give a design update to fashionable containers, such as terracotta pots. For the dipping method described on this page, only a terracotta pot is suitable.

DIPPING

1 Take a container large enough to hold the pot that is to be coloured and almost fill it with cold water. Using an aerosol spray paint, spray the chosen colour on the top of the water to form a thick layer of paint. Almost straight away, dip the pot (or plant materials) in the container and carefully remove it. (To ensure a good coverage of paint, dip the container immediately; if the paint is left on the water too long it will form a skin.) Leave to dry.

2 To produce a realistic finish, small strips of soft pliable lead are folded over the rim of the container.

PROFESSIONAL TIP

Remember, never use a spray paint, varnish or other paint in an enclosed room. Always ensure that good ventilation. People with breathing problems must be very cautious and read the manufacturer's instructions carefully.

Silvered ivy flowers and pebbles add a magical touch to this design of amaryllis lilies and fruit.

OTHER EFFECTS

A red sandstone effect can be created by painting a wooden pedestal or similar container with a mixture of red and brown emulsions and then, while the paint is still wet, sprinkling handfuls of coarse red sand over it. Marbling is a skilled paint effect, but one worth acquiring, as it can be used to turn humble wood stands and containers into elegant 'marble'.

Index

Advent
colours, 13
Glowing Advent Crown, 118
see also Christmas
Aftercare advice, 147
Aqua-packing, 78, 92, 146
Arch, floral, Glistening
Droplets, 138
Artificial flowers
Lasting Wall Decoration,
24-25
Making an entrance, 82
Autumn, bouquet, 70-72

Bacteria, 147
Basket arrangements
Basket of Orchard
Delights, 16-17
Summer Scents for a
Bridesmaid, 66-67
Blocks, designer, 39
Boundaries, Extending the,
126-143
Bouquets
bride's vision of, 59
Cascade of Lilac and Lilies,
60-61
Experimental Bouquet,
140-141
Glorious Bouquet, 80-81
Purple Haze, 70-72
Rainbow-Wrapped Roses,
94-95
Sparkling Fresh Handtied,
92-93
Summer Waterfall, 66
techniques, 152-153
Winter Wedding, 74-75
see also Posies
Bowl, Rococo, 34-35
Box arrangement, 32-33
Bridy holder, 152
Bucket cleaners, 145
Business functions
Arrangement for, 108

Corporate Launch, 110-111
Buying cut materials, 144,
148-151

Cages, 35, 152
Candle arrangements,
Summer Dream, 104-106,
118-119
Candles, 101
Care of cut flowers, 144-151
Casket covering design, 40-41
Cellophane, 92, 94-95
Chaplets, sympathy tributes,
44
Checklist for events, 101
Choices for weddings, 58
Christmas
colours, 13, 94
Stable Door, 142-143
Twelve Days of Christmas,
122-123
White and Lime Christmas,
120-121
see also Advent
Clay pots, using, 134-135
College of Horticulture,
Welsh, 7-8
Colours
choosing, 12-13
experimenting with, 127
schemes for weddings, 59
Combinations
of colours, 12
flowers and fruit, 16
Conditioning materials,
priorities/methods,
145-146
Cone wrapping, 88
Containers
covered, 156
for Flemish flower
paintings, 28
foliage as, 26
paint effects, 157
Copper tubing, Copper

Curves, 20
Coverings for containers, 156
Crests *see* Logos
Crosses, sympathy tributes, 44
Cushions
and pillows, difference, 44
sympathy designs, 39
Cut flowers, care of, 144-151
Cutting stems, 145

Days, special, colours for, 13
Decorations, positioning, 100
Decorative arrangements,
12-35
Designer
blocks, 39
sheets, 39, 46-47
Designs
free-standing floor, 102-103,
110-111
influences from Europe, 6-7
innovative, 126
sympathy, 39
Desks, reception, 79, 82
Dipping, paint effect, 157
Dried flowers
Lasting Wall Decoration,
24-25
Making an Entrance, 82
Drinking times, 146

Easter, colours, 13
Emblems see Logos
Ethylene gas, 146-147
Euphorbias, professional
tips, 63
Europe, influences from, 6-7
European sympathy spray, 39
Events
logos for, 39
planning, 100
Special, Schemes, 100-123

Fabrics
and flowers, weddings, 59

as overlays, 106
Fashion
colours in, 13
trends, 6
Festivals, colours for, 13
Flemish flower paintings, 28
Floor designs
Corporate Launch, 110-111
Free Expression, 102-103
Flower food, 147
and plastic foam, 108
Foliage as container,
The Rainforest, 26-27
Food for flowers, 108, 147
Forms of arrangements, 126
Frames, 152-153
bamboo, 80-81
funeral tributes, 38
of twigs, 35, 88-89, 132-133
Framing, design technique, 85
Fruit and flower
combinations, 16
Functions *see* Events
Funeral tributes, 38-55, 79

Garlands, Floral Passion,
68-69
Gifts
bouquets, Sparkling Fresh
Handtied, 92-93
Mother's Day Delights,
32-35
One of Life's Pleasures,
30-31
Rainbow-Wrapped Roses,
94-95
Valentine's, 78, 90
Glue gun, 25
Grass, weaving, 155
Guidelines for handtieds, 79

Handtieds
bouquets, Cascade of Lilac
and Lilies, 60-61
ideas for, 78-97

posies, Spring Bridesmaid,
62-63
Harvest time
colours, 13
Cornucopia, 14
Hearts
Romantically Inclined,
78, 90
sympathy tributes, 44
Horticulture, Welsh College
of, 7-8
Hospitals, colours for, 12, 13

Impact, creating, 100
Inspection of cut materials,
144-145

Jug tapestry, 136-137, 156

Lead
Cornucopia, 14
Mango Colours in a Lead
Cone, 88-89
Walk on the Wild Side,
128-129
Lighting, 101
Lines of arrangements,
126-127
Logos
business/sporting, 39
Fleur de Lys, 46-47
Scottish Thistle, 50-51

Marbling, 157
Minimalist style, Mango
Colours in a Lead Cone,
88-89
Moss sculpture, 130
Mother's Day
arrangements, 32-35
colours, 13

Over-binding,
choice of materials, 153
methods, 153

Paint effects, 157
Paintings of flowers, 28
Palms, plaiting, 154
Paper wrapping, 94-95
Parties
Children's, 112
Pure Fantasy, 116
Scottish theme, 50
themes, 100, 104
Pedestal arrangements
Classical English Pedestal, 22
designs, 100
Harvest Moon, 18
Photocopies for designs, 46
Pillows
and cushions, difference, 44
sympathy designs, 39
Textured Pillow, 44
Plaiting palms, 154
Planning events, 100
Plastic wrapping, 92, 94-95
Posies, handtied
Captured Roses, 84-85
Mermaid Posy, 78, 86
Spring Bridesmaid, 62-63
Positions of decorations, 100
Preparation
of cut materials, 144
research, 51

Reception desks, 79, 82
Research, 51
Restaurant tables, 79
Rules for handtieds, 79

Sandstone effect, 157
Schemes for special events,
100-123
Sculptures
Moss Sculpture, 130
Walk on the Wild Side,
128-129
Seasons, colours for, 13
Service, efficient, for
bereaved, 38

Shapes of arrangements, 126
Sheets, designer, 39, 46-47
Shop displays, 102
Sight, poor, colours for
people with, 12
Skills, 58-59
Space for arrangements, 127
Sprays, Thoughts of a Spring
Meadow, 48-49
Stages
decoration, 111
setting, 102
Stems, cutting, 145
Storage of flowers, 146
Styles, 6
futuristic 96
minimalist, 88-89
Superstitions and colours, 12
Sympathy designs, 38-55, 79

Table arrangements, 100
Positive Charge, 134-135
restaurant, 79
Summer Dream, 104-106
Christmas, 122-123
Tape for support grids, 28
Tapestry effect, 136-137, 156
Techniques, 58-59, 152-157
framing, 85
innovative techniques for
handtieds, 78
Temperatures for storage, 146
Templates, 46
Textures, 127
Themes for parties, 50, 100,
104, 116
Thistles
Scottish, Thistle, 50-51
sympathy designs, 39
Tributes, funeral, 38-55, 79
Tubes
copper, 20, 142-143
plastic mesh, 68
Twigs
Blue Vortex, 132-133

frameworks, 35, 88-89
Woven Beauty, 54-55

Valentine's Day
colours, 13
Romantically Inclined, 78, 90
Vase life of cut flowers,
148-151
Venues for events, 100-101
Versatility of handtieds, 78-79

Wall decorations
Lasting Wall Decoration,
24-25
see also Garlands
Weaving
Anthurium Swirl, 136-137
Blue Vortex, 132-133
in a framework, 88-89
grass, 155
twigs, 54-55
Weddings
anniversaries, 100
Floral, 58-75
Flower Border, 114-115
handtieds for, 78-79
Welsh College of Horticulture,
7-8
Whitsun, colours, 13
Winter bouquet, 74-75
Work plans for events, 101
Wrapping paper/plastic, 92,
94-95
Wreaths
Christmas, 142
Eternal Circle, 42-43
for Glorious Bouquet, 80
holly, as memorials, 38
Swirling Cluster Wreath,
52-53

ACKNOWLEDGEMENTS

This book has been completed with the help and encouragement of family, friends, colleagues and especially those mentioned below: Dr Mark Simkin, Principal, for the use of the extensive floristry facilities and the beautiful gardens of the Welsh College of Horticulture; Karen Hemingway, Commissioning Editor of Merehurst, for her hard work on the book and patience with us; Diana Lodge, our supportive and encouraging editor – we couldn't have done it without you; Jane Forster, designer, whose skills contribute such a lot to the book, and Karl Adamson, our marvellous photographer - you were great! Many thanks, also, to Ian Lloyd, who so willingly gave his time and expertise; Jo Green and Paul Raven, two special people who have designs on several pages, and our students from 1997, who enjoyed the extra work and contributed their time and talents. Finally, our thanks to Amanda Kenny and her staff at the Celyn Plant Centre. We would also like to thank the following companies for supplying their products: Smithers Oasis UK Ltd, Naylor Bases Ltd, Chrysal Ltd, Val Spicer Designs, The Flower Shop (Northwich), the Flower Council of Holland, and Guernsey Flowers.

First published in 1998 by Merehurst Limited
Ferry House, 51-57 Lacy Road, Putney, London SW15 1PR
Copyright © 1998 Merehurst Limited

ISBN 1-85391-517-3

A catalogue record of this book is available from the British Library.

Commissioning Editor: Karen Hemingway
Editor: Diana Lodge
Designer: Jane Forster
Photographer: Karl Adamson

CEO & Publisher: Anne Wilson
International Sales Director: Mark Newman

Colour separation by Bright Arts (HK) Limited
Printed in Singapore by CS Graphics